It Happened to Me

Series Editor: Arlene Hirschfelder

Books in the "It Happened to Me" series are designed for inquisitive teens digging for answers about certain illnesses, social issues, or lifestyle interests. Whether you are deep into your teen years or just entering them, these books are gold mines of up-to-date information, riveting teen views, and great visuals to help you figure out stuff. Besides special boxes highlighting singular facts, each book is enhanced with the latest reading list, websites, and an index. Perfect for browsing, there's loads of expert information by acclaimed writers to help parents, guardians, and librarians understand teen illness, tough situations, and lifestyle choices.

1. *Learning Disabilities: The Ultimate Teen Guide,* by Penny Hutchins Paquette and Cheryl Gerson Tuttle, 2002.
2. *Epilepsy: The Ultimate Teen Guide,* by Kathlyn Gay and Sean McGarrahan, 2002.
3. *Stress Relief: The Ultimate Teen Guide,* by Mark Powell, 2002.
4. *Making Sexual Decisions: The Ultimate Teen Guide,* by L. Kris Gowen, Ph.D., 2003.
5. *Asthma: The Ultimate Teen Guide,* by Penny Hutchins Paquette, 2003.
6. *Cultural Diversity: Conflicts and Challenges: The Ultimate Teen Guide,* by Kathlyn Gay, 2003.

Cultural Diversity: Conflicts and Challenges

The Ultimate Teen Guide

KATHLYN GAY

It Happened to Me, No. 6

The Scarecrow Press, Inc.
Lanham, Maryland, and Oxford
2003

SCARECROW PRESS, INC.

Published in the United States of America
by Scarecrow Press, Inc.
A Member of the Rowman & Littlefield Publishing Group
4501 Forbes Boulevard, Suite 200, Lanham, Maryland 20706
www.scarecrowpress.com

PO Box 317
Oxford
OX2 9RU, UK

British Library Cataloguing in Publication Information Available

Library of Congress Cataloging-in-Publication Data

Gay, Kathlyn.
Cultural diversity : conflicts and challenges : the ultimate teen guide / Kathlyn Gay.
v. cm.—(It happened to me ; no. 6)
Includes bibliographical references and index.
Contents: Out of many, one?—Challenges in a diverse society—Prejudice and racism amidst diversity—Racist images and stereotypes—Religious diversity and conflicts—From intolerance to hatred to violence—Reducing bigotry, racism, and hate crimes—Respecting diversity—Speaking out.
ISBN 0-8108-4805-8 (pbk. : alk. paper)
1. Pluralism (Social sciences)—Juvenile literature. 2. Toleration—Juvenile literature. 3. Racism—Juvenile literature. 4. Prejudices—Juvenile literature. 5. Pluralism (Social Sciences)—United States—Juvenile literature. 6. Toleration—United States—Juvenile literature. 7. Racism—United States—Juvenile literature. [1. Pluralism (Social sciences) 2. Toleration. 3. Prejudices. 4. Racism.] I. Title. II. Series.
HM1271 .G39 2003
305.8—dc21 2003007709

∞™ The paper used in this publication meets the minimum requirements of American National Standard for Information Sciences—Permanence of Paper for Printed Library Materials, ANSI/NISO Z39.48-1992.
Manufactured in the United States of America.

Contents

1 Out of Many, One? 1

Hatred Alive and Well 2
Diversity Issues 3
From the "Melting Pot" to the "Tossed Salad" 4
Becoming Part of the Tossed Salad 8

2 Challenges in a Diverse Society 11

Being "Politically Correct" 13
Language and Lifestyle Challenges 16

3 Prejudice and Racism Amid Diversity 21

Prejudice 22
Sexual Prejudice 24
Harassment and Attacks at Schools 25
About Race and Racism 26
What Is Race? 27
What Is Racism? 28
What Keeps Prejudice and Racism Alive? 30
"White Privilege" 33
Scapegoats for Economic Problems 34

4 Racist Images and Stereotypes 37

Racist Images of Native Peoples 37
Insulting Indian Icons 40
Black Stereotypes 42
In and Out of the Picture 45
Asian American and Latino Caricatures 46
More Negative Stereotypes 47

5 Religious Diversity and Conflicts 51

The First and Fourteenth Amendments 51
Bigotry or Statements of Faith? 55
Religious Diversity in Public Schools 57
An Ongoing Issue 58
Politics and Religious Diversity 60

6 From Intolerance, to Hatred, to Violence 63

Some Hatemongers 66
White Aryan Resistance 68
Turning Teenagers on to Hate 70

7 Reducing Bigotry, Racism, and Hate Crimes 75

Anytown USA 76
Day of Silence 78
Not in Our Town 79
More Groups at Work 81
Effective State and Local Groups 83

8 Respecting Diversity 87
Can *We All Get Along?* 87
Understanding Differences 91

9 Speaking Out 95

Finding a Voice 96

Chapter Notes 101

Glossary 111

For Further Information 113

Index 117

About the Author 121

1 Out of Many, One?

I'm Arabic, my family is Arabic, some of my family [are] Muslim . . . and we're all being treated as if we are terrorists. I am an American.

—Florida teenager

"I am an American" was the theme of a television commercial and ad campaign released in late September 2001 by the Ad Council, which provides free public service messages for the media. The commercial underscored the nation's creed, "*E Pluribus Unum*" (Out of Many, One). People of various ages, skin colors, and occupations repeated the four words, "I am an American," simply and dramatically celebrating the nation's diversity and at the same time encouraging unity.

Why was the ad campaign created? Not long after Arab terrorists attacked the World Trade Center (WTC) in New York City and the Pentagon near Washington, D.C., on September 11, 2001, many Arab Americans, Muslims, and Asian Americans with dark skin, hair, and eyes became targets for blame. They were stereotyped, seen as part of a group rather than being recognized as individuals, and erroneously viewed as responsible for thousands of deaths. As a teenager in Florida put it, "I'm Arabic, my family is Arabic, some of my family [are] Muslim, I have Arabic friends, and we're all being treated as if we are terrorists. I am an American. I was born here so this is my country. . . . I have an excellent heritage, but I am American. It's ironic that this new prejudice is against those who love this country."[1]

Check it out!
A stereotype is a fixed idea about a particular group; seeing a person as part of a group rather than as an individual.

The Ad Council launched its campaign to help counteract the prejudice, stereotypes, and hate, which have affected individuals in communities across the United States. "Americans need to unite and embrace our diversity as a nation now more than ever . . . we must work together to protect all Americans from hate crimes and violence," states Ad Council president Peggy Conlon.[2]

Hatred Alive and Well

In spite of the ad campaign message, prejudice and hate appear to be alive and well. Not only are there anti-Arab and anti-Muslim attacks, but anti-Semitism is on the rise as well.

Since January 2002, anti-Semitic attacks have escalated in the United States, in European countries (primarily France and Germany), and in Canada and Argentina. Incidents include graffiti and vandalism of Jewish synagogues and temples, hate speech, and violence, which are prompted in part by the conflict between Palestinians and Israelis in the Middle East.

Check it out!

Anti-Semitism is hatred and prejudice against Jewish people or Judaism.

Numerous pro-Palestinian rallies have been held in U.S. cities, among them New York City, San Francisco,

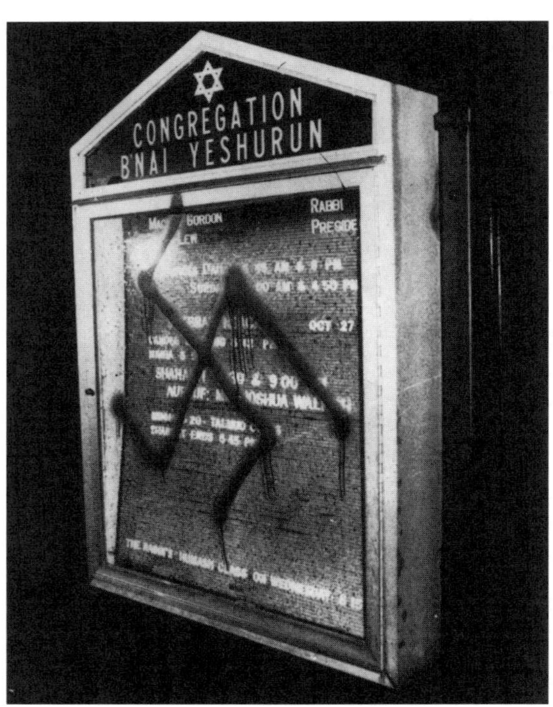

Anti-Semitic acts often include vandalism of Jewish synagogues and temples. Photo courtesy of the Anti-Defamation League.

Chicago, Detroit, and Washington, D.C. However, the rallies have turned into forums for spewing hatred against Jews and Israel, according to the Anti-Defamation League, which fights anti-Semitism throughout the world. Posters and fliers distributed at the rallies "refer to the 'genocide' of the Palestinian people, suggesting that Israel has adopted a policy similar to Nazi Germany's program to exterminate the Jews of Europe during the Holocaust. The Holocaust, and Holocaust imagery such as the swastika, is constantly evoked at pro-Palestinian rallies, often in a manner that is deeply offensive to Jews and especially Holocaust survivors."[3]

More than one hundred anti-Semitic incidents occurred on U.S. college campuses between January and May 2002. In April, for example, about fifty San Francisco State University students, who had attended a rally calling for peace in the Middle East, were surrounded by a mob of Muslim demonstrators shouting, "Kill the Jews!" "Hitler didn't finish the job," and "Get out or we'll kill you!" Similar demonstrations have been held at the University of California, Berkeley campus. At both universities, legal actions have been taken to stop anti-Semitic demonstrations.

DIVERSITY ISSUES

Obviously, efforts to unify Americans and encourage acceptance of diverse views are not easy tasks, especially when deep hatreds trigger violence. But to achieve the motto of *E Pluribus Unum,* organizations, groups, and individuals across the United States attempt to deal with diversity issues that crop up daily in schools, on the job, in neighborhoods, within families, in the courts, and in many other institutions and situations.

Some diversity issues are related to gender—that is, conflicts over whether individuals should have to accept defined roles for what females and males can do and how they should behave. As Chicago teenager Cierra Benton puts it, "One type of stereotyping I see and can relate to is young women and sports. Boys underestimate girls' ability to play

DIVERSITY ISSUES WITHIN A FAMILY

Diversity issues frequently affect so-called mixed-race families, whether formed biologically by interracial couples or by parents who adopt children whose racial ancestry is not the same as their own. Since the 1960s and 1970s, the number of mixed families has steadily increased. But that does not mean that such families are readily accepted in every community. One anonymous teenager living in "a typical suburban neighborhood" where "faces of color are few and far between," writes that as a "young, white female" she had "never experienced racism firsthand." However, because her adopted brother is of Asian ancestry she saw "how people react to those who are of a different color." She explains:

> ***My brother is 17 years old and has always lived in a predominantly white neighborhood where he attends a predominantly white school. He was adopted from Korea when he was two months old. . . . America is the only [country] he has ever known. That doesn't stop people from asking him if he misses [Korea]. When asked this question, his eyebrows perk up and he becomes automatically confused and says, "But, I am home."***
>
> ***At other times, people have asked such questions as, "Got any rice?"***
>
> ***He has been referred to by many utterly offensive names. Since he is Asian, people assumed he is really smart and can't pronounce his R's. People mock his height and the way his eyes are shaped.[4]***

ball and they think that we are just so delicate and we can't do anything physical, and I do find it offensive because I do not like to be underestimated because I am a female."[5]

Other issues arise because of attempts to include people with physical disabilities in school classes, on jobs, and in social activities. Sexual orientation is also an issue: people may be excluded, discriminated against, harassed, or attacked because they happen to be gay or lesbian.

For the most part, though, conflicts come about because of cultural differences. The United States is one of the most diverse nations in the world, home to people who have come from almost every part of the globe and brought with them their cultural patterns: that is, ways of communicating, dress, food customs, and various holiday traditions.

FROM THE "MELTING POT" TO THE "TOSSED SALAD"

The United States is frequently referred to as a nation of immigrants. During the 1800s and early 1900s, millions of people emigrated, primarily from Europe, to the United States. These new arrivals were expected to give up their original

SHARING A CULTURE

People of any given ethnic group usually share a common culture—traditions, religious beliefs, and usually a basic language, all of which provide structure for and give meaning to their lives. It was common in the past and is still true today that members of an ethnic group often live in the same neighborhood of a city or town. "I have great memories of my years growing up in a south suburb of Chicago," says Dean Hamilton whose family included first-generation Italians on his mother's side. While he was in high school during the late 1950s, "our community was 99 percent Italian and black—there were very few whites. Italians didn't consider themselves white but of course they were not black either," he explains.

Hamilton notes that in the four-year high school he attended, there was not a lot of friction until "upper-middle-class white kids from another suburb were sent to our school—their school system didn't have room for them. That's when real segregation happened—the new kids kept to themselves—they didn't participate in activities, they didn't want to be there." He acknowledges that "Italian and black kids didn't always get along—we'd trade insults with each other—but there wasn't such a line or barrier as there sometimes is today. In fact, I dated a black girl during that time."

Although an ethnic community can sometimes seem "pretty closed," Hamilton recalls "a lifestyle that many native-born Americans never experience, such as speaking another language other than English. Everybody who came to our house spoke Italian, with the exception of my father who wasn't Italian and never really learned the language."

Hamilton says that it was tradition in his household for the whole family to eat dinner together and he has fond memories of holiday cooking:

> *There was a lot of emphasis on Christmas and Easter because of our Catholic background. We always had fish—shrimp, smelt, calamari—on Christmas eve, for example, which is traditional Italian. Sometimes today, when I go to a real Italian restaurant, I get an instant flashback of what it was like when I was growing up. Everything was made at home—sauce and pasta. Pasta would hang from curtain rods drying. No one ever bought cookies. They were all baked at home. My grandmother, who taught herself how to speak English, made ricotta cheese and sold some of it from the house—her small business.*

After he became an adult, Hamilton says that people who knew nothing about his Italian background were fascinated with his heritage. "They wanted to learn about it." Today, he says, "communication—talking to one another—is one of the best ways to break down cultural barriers. We can't go through life with blinders on."[6]

customs and be absorbed or assimilated into the predominant way of life established by white Anglo-Saxon (of northern European extraction) Protestants (WASPs). This meant immigrants accepted, for the most part, the Protestant view of morality, respect for law and order, duty to work for a living, and appreciation of democratic institutions, including public

DIVERSITY ISSUES IN THE NEWS

Headlines from recent magazine and newspaper articles represent a sampling of the cultural diversity issues that are being raised nationwide:

- **Gay Teens Ignored by High School Sex Ed Classes—*Women's Enews***
- **Abercrombie & Fitch Pulls Asian Caricature T-Shirts Amid Protests—Associated Press**
- **Indian Identity Is Important Subject—*Indian Country Today***
- **Study Looks at Black Skin Stereotypes—Associated Press**
- **Diversity Lags in Most Newsrooms—Associated Press**
- **Police Agencies Improve, Slowly, in Dealing with Cultural Collisions—Knight Ridder News Service**
- **"Workers, Go Home!" (The Anti-Immigrant Movement)—*Christian Century***
- **White Supremacists Meet in York, PA—Associated Press**
- **Cultural Clashes in the Workplace—*Houston Chronicle***
- **Race Discussions Seek to Root out Discrimination—*Orlando Sentinel***

schools. Teachers taught their students not only the English language, but also how to blend in and become part of the American "melting pot."[7]

The melting pot idea was widely accepted until the 1960s and 1970s, when the civil rights movement called attention to the fact that throughout U.S. history many groups have been deliberately excluded. The nation's past is full of strategies and legal practices used to reject most nonwhites and also many non-Christians.

Check it out!

There are differing views on where and how the "melting pot" term came into being. Some historians believe it was coined—or at least became popular—when Israel Zangwill, a European immigrant, wrote a play while aboard a ship to America. Titled *The Melting Pot*, the play opened in Washington, D.C., in 1908. But others claim the concept of a melting pot had been discussed long before that in 1782 when J. Hector de Crevecoeur, a Frenchman who settled in New York, described the United States as a society in which individuals of all nations are melted into a new "race" of people.

"KEEP OUT!"

From colonial times, many groups of Americans have been excluded from the melting pot. To begin with, only a few colonies welcomed people of religious faiths different from their own. Those who did not conform to an established religion were harassed, persecuted, or killed.

As the nation expanded, indigenous people (sometimes called American Indians or Native Americans) were forced off their land and sent to reservations, with thousands dying on the way. Black Americans were enslaved and for decades after emancipation were separated by law from whites in schools, the military, in restaurants, offices, and courts, and in most other public facilities.

During the 1800s, native-born Americans, mostly WASPs, called for restrictions on immigration of Roman Catholic Irish. Nativists, as they were called, resented the Irish for their poverty and clannish ways. In addition, Protestants feared what they called the "Catholic menace" and frequently incited anti-Catholic riots. They also opposed the influx of emigrants from southern Europe, agreeing with a journalist who wrote that "[t]he American nation was founded and developed by the Nordic race, but if a few more million members of the Alpine, Mediterranean and Semitic races are poured among us, the result must inevitably be a hybrid race of people as worthless and futile as the good-for-nothing mongrels of Central America and Southeast Europe."[8]

Chinese immigrants were also shown the "keep out!" sign, even though they had been recruited to work on the transcontinental railroad during the late 1800s. When an economic depression hit, labor leaders accused the Chinese of taking jobs that Americans needed and claimed that Chinese "immigrants were socially and morally inferior to whites and that as a separate race they could never be assimilated into American society."[9]

During World War II, American citizens of Japanese ancestry were relocated from the West Coast to inland concentration camps. In spite of dedication to their country, thousands of Japanese Americans lost their land, businesses, homes, and personal property. Not until 1987 were Japanese Americans provided a token sum (about $20,000 each) for their losses.

From about the mid-1950s to the present, white supremacists have preached doctrines of exclusion. The Ku Klux Klan, neo-Nazis, Aryan Nations, Skinheads, Christian Identity, and hundreds of other groups have spread their hate messages and committed numerous violent attacks against nonwhites, Jews, homosexuals, and others they consider "undesirable."

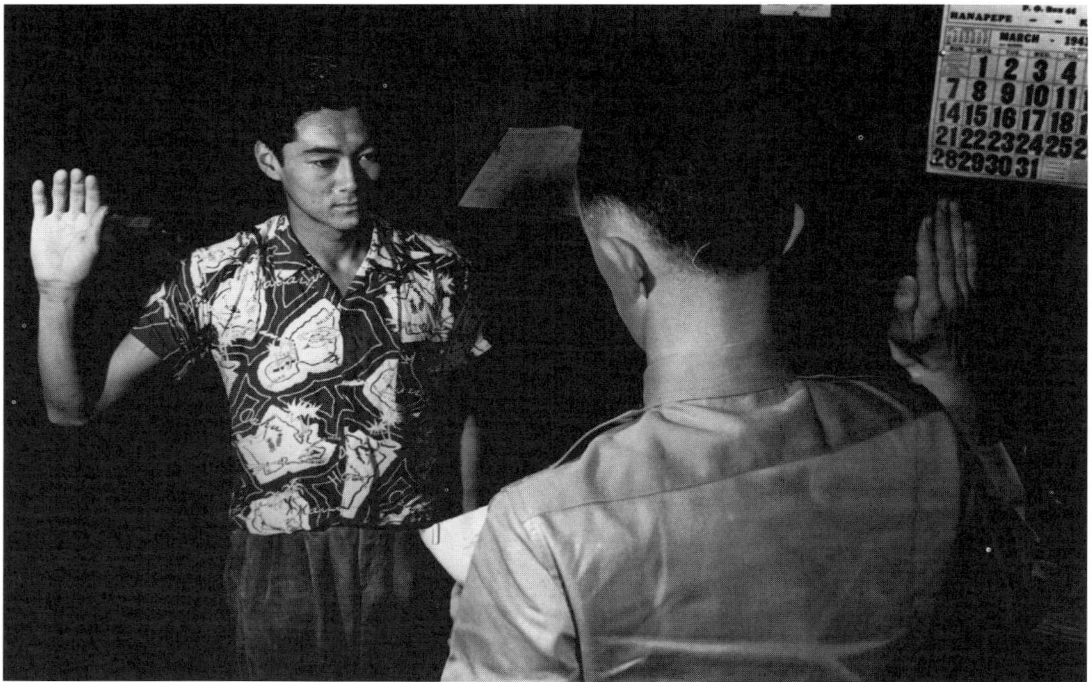

During World War II, numerous Japanese Americans volunteered to serve in the armed forces, in spite of discrimination against them and internment of Japanese Americans in U.S. concentration camps. In this photo, eighteen-year-old Mitsuru Doi of Japanese ancestry takes an oath of induction into the U.S. Army. Photo courtesy of the Library of Congress.

By the 1970s, the idea of and respect for cultural or ethnic pluralism began to take shape in the United States. Cultural pluralism means that various ethnic groups maintain some of their original traditions and social customs but also adopt aspects of the dominant lifestyle.

The concept of cultural pluralism or cultural diversity replaces the melting pot image with what is frequently described as a "mosaic" or a "tossed salad." As Christine I. Bennett of Indiana University explains, "Each part retains some of its uniqueness while contributing to the beauty and strength of the whole composition."[10]

BECOMING PART OF THE TOSSED SALAD

Ameesha Nanwani of Great Neck (New York) North High School emigrated from India and even after living in the

United States for twelve years felt more Indian than American. When the WTC terrorist attacks occurred, however, Ameesha's attitude changed. "It was surprising to care so much about America. I knew in the back of my mind that if anything were to start in America I always had the opportunity to leave and go live in my house in India, but now I did not want to." In an award-winning essay, Ameesha writes:

> *On Friday, September 14, [2001] my friends and I went to a bridge in our town where a vigil for the missing was held. There were five of us: one Indian (myself), one Colombian, one Russian, one Israeli, and the last one from China. We all stood in a line in front of the candles and said a prayer in six different languages: English, Hindi, Cantonese, Russian, Spanish, and Hebrew, for two victims—one Greek-American trader and one Italian-American fireman. We were no longer segregated by petty differences. We came together as one unit from different countries and cultures as Americans supporting our country. It was the most intense moment of my life. . . . I realized that I am an American as well as an Indian, and . . . that being an American does not mean that you have to give up your culture and roots. Being an American allows you to embrace them and share them with everyone around you regardless of their origin or nationality.*[11]

2 Challenges in a Diverse Society

Greetings! I am pleased to see that we are different. May we together become greater than the sum of both of us.

—A Vulcan greeting from the TV series *Star Trek*

Although many Americans tout the benefits of a culturally diverse society, some contend that an emphasis on ethnic uniqueness or ethnic identity polarizes Americans and threatens the survival of the nation. In other words, critics say, if members of a particular ethnic group maintain their culture, they will not be loyal, patriotic Americans. An example of this view appeared in an editorial, which circulated widely via e-mail and on websites in early 2002. Supposedly, the piece was first printed in a Florida newspaper, but the name and date of the newspaper and the name of the writer were not revealed. The anonymous writer declares that a "multicultural community has served only to dilute our sovereignty and our national identity" and asserts that immigrants "and apparently some born here" need to understand that Americans have their own culture, language, and lifestyle. Furthermore, the writer states:

> *We speak ENGLISH, not Spanish, Arabic, Chinese, Japanese, Russian, or any other language. Therefore, if you wish to become part of our society, learn the language!*
>
> *"In God We Trust" is our national motto. This is not some Christian, right wing, political slogan. We adopted this motto because Christian men and women, on Christian principles, founded this nation, and this is clearly documented. It is certainly appropriate to display it on the walls of our schools. If God offends you, then I suggest you consider another part of the world as your new home, because God is part of our culture. If Stars and Stripes offend you, or you don't like Uncle Sam, then you should seriously consider a move to another part of this planet. . . . This is OUR COUNTRY, our land, and*

our lifestyle. Our First Amendment gives every citizen the right to express his opinion and we will allow you every opportunity to do so. But, once you are done complaining, whining, and griping about our flag, our pledge, our national motto, or our way of life, I highly encourage you to take advantage of one other great American freedom, THE RIGHT TO LEAVE.[1]

REBUTTAL

A search on the Internet reveals very few rebuttals to the anonymous love-it-or-leave-it editorial, but one came from Kara who wrote:

I got this e-mail forwarded to me the other day. I started reading it and immediately thought, "Yeah! Tell it like it is!" . . . Then, after I'd had a chance to digest it all, I realized how very wrong it is. . . . We are a multicultural nation and I am thankful for it. Try to deny it all you want, but that is "our" culture. . . . I must say that not only are we Americans multicultural, but we are also multilingual. . . . Thousands of words we use everyday in the English language came directly from other languages. I'm not talking about words that we adapted and changed. I'm talking about words that we use exactly as they are used in the countries they hail from. The word "baby" is Dutch, "squirrel" is French, "cotton" is Arabic, "safari" is Swahili, "sauna" is Finnish, "kindergarten" is German, and "pajamas" is Indian. Was it un-American of us to adopt these foreign words, along with thousands of others, into our language? I certainly hope not because it would be a real shame if we had to give them all back.[2]

The writer asks people to pass on the message, if they agree with the expressed opinions. Hundreds, perhaps thousands, of e-mail users and Internet surfers did just that. But some people refused to circulate what appears to be a personal rant that is factually flawed.

The views expressed in the anonymous editorial are not new. For decades, the idea that the United States is basically a "Christian" nation and that everyone trusts in God has been challenged repeatedly. As Baptist theologian R. P. Nettelhorst, a professor of the Bible and biblical languages, writes, "Many well-meaning Christians argue that the United States was founded by Christian men on Christian principles. Although well-intentioned, such sentiment is unfounded. The men who led the United States in its revolution against England, who wrote the Declaration of Independence and put together the Constitution were not Christians by any stretch of the imagination."[3]

Published documents show that the nation's founders may have believed in God, but most were deists or Unitarians who did not accept Christian tenets.

Thomas Paine, a deist whose pamphlet *Common Sense* inspired many colonists to fight for independence in the American Revolution, declared, "I do not believe in the creed professed by the Jewish church, by the Roman church, by the Greek church, by the Turkish church, by the Protestant church, nor by any church that I know of. My mind is my own church."[4]

Check it out!

A deist is a person who rejects formal religion and supernatural revelations and instead contends that nature reveals the existence of God.

John Adams, the second U.S. president and a Unitarian, did not believe in the deity of Christ. During his presidency, the U.S. Senate in 1797 ratified a peace treaty with the Islamic government of Tripoli, and Article 11 of the treaty begins, "the government of the United States of America is not in any sense founded on the Christian Religion."[5]

Thomas Jefferson, author of the Declaration of Independence and the third U.S. president, was "a confirmed deist who believed in natural religion and morality."[6] Jefferson frequently expressed his views in his prolific writings.

"IN GOD WE TRUST"

The motto "In God We Trust" has sparked controversy in recent times. According to the U.S. Treasury Department, the motto was placed on currency because of political pressure and "increased religious sentiment" during the Civil War. People were concerned about the fate of the Union and sought divine protection. "Secretary of the Treasury Salmon P. Chase received many appeals from devout persons throughout the country, urging that the United States recognize the Deity on United States coins."[7]

Various coins carried the motto off and on throughout the nineteenth century and into the next. Then, in 1956 the U.S. Congress issued a joint resolution, which was approved by President Dwight D. Eisenhower, declaring "In God We Trust" the national motto of the United States.

BEING "POLITICALLY CORRECT"

As the United States has become increasingly diverse, political correctness (PC) has been challenged by numerous critics. PC has a great variety of meanings, but basically it is a belief that people of diverse cultures should be treated with respect by not using terminology and taking actions that offend them. Some advocates contend that PC helps Americans be more tolerant of one another. For example, the term "cripple" is seldom used in news reports today because it is considered a derogatory way to describe a person with a physical disability. "Fit" is an inappropriate way to describe a "seizure," the accurate term for someone who experiences the effects of a neurological disorder. The list could go on for pages, but the point is that attempts are made to avoid using terms that are associated with negative stereotypes.

On the other hand, some critics believe that PC hampers free speech. As Kate, a teenager in Akron, Ohio, puts it, "How can we speak our minds if we are always trying to make sure we don't offend anyone?" Writing for *Teen Ink,* Kate notes, "It seems like people today nitpick. . . . Whether it is a billboard, speech or a picture, someone will say it is offensive or discriminatory. This is as wrong as discrimination, and people should be able to speak their minds and represent themselves without being concerned with political correctness."[8]

Debates over PC are ongoing and one example was the controversy that erupted in early 2002 when a bronze statue was commissioned by the Brooklyn, New York, Fire Department. Designed to pay tribute to the 343 firefighters killed in the September 11, 2001, attack on the World Trade Center, the proposed statue was based on a famous photograph showing three white firefighters raising a U.S. flag on the rubble. But the statue included one white, one black, and one Hispanic firefighter. According to a report on CNN in January 2002, critics thought the design was

> *political correctness run amok and an attempt to rewrite history. . . . The decision to represent different races was made by the Fire Department, the makers of the statue, and the property-management company that owns the department headquarters building and commissioned the work. "Given that those who died were of all races and*

Interracial/intercultural groups frequently meet at conferences across the United States to discuss diversity issues. Photo by the author.

> *all ethnicities and that the statue was to be symbolic of those sacrifices, ultimately a decision was made to honor no one in particular, but everyone who made the supreme sacrifice," fire department spokesman Frank Gribbon said.*[9]

Teenager Stephanie W. weighs in on the proposed statue when she writes in *Teen Ink:*

> *In my opinion, we should show the moment as it happened. By changing the faces, we are changing history. If one really wants to be politically correct, then there should be a woman. But that's uncalled for, right?*
>
> *There was no woman helping to raise the flag. But there were no African Americans or Hispanics raising that flag, either. It goes without saying that African Americans and Hispanics died that tragic day. But there*

were also women, children, disabled people and many, many others. America is diverse, and always will be. We don't need to change history to know that.[10]

Such criticism from numerous sources, including complaints from the firefighters in the photograph of the flag raising, led officials to look for another design. Nevertheless, others support the idea that a statue, like various art forms, can represent a historical event without literally reconstructing it.

LANGUAGE AND LIFESTYLE CHALLENGES

Along with other diversity issues, language and lifestyle differences can create challenges, especially as an increasing number of immigrants arrive in the United States. "The foreign-born are now 10 percent of the U.S. population," Kenneth Prewitt reports in the *Brookings Review.* "The proportion itself is not remarkable; numbers that high were common in the late 19th and early 20th centuries." But newcomers today are not predominately European as they were in the past. Rather they are "Asian, Latin American, Caribbean, Middle Eastern, and African."[11]

Many of the recent immigrants are refugees from Afghanistan, Bosnia, Iraq, Laos, Sudan, and the former Soviet Union; they have escaped war, persecution, torture, or extreme poverty—sometimes all of the above. Refugees often settle on the East or West Coasts, but a large number have migrated to such midwestern states as Nebraska, Iowa, and Minnesota.

One group of recent arrivals to the United States emigrated from Somalia and settled in Minnesota under the sponsorship of church-related organizations. Many of the newcomers are also refugees and live in Owatonna, a city of twenty thousand south of Minneapolis. Somalian students, who range in age from sixteen to twenty, attend classes at Owatonna Senior High School to learn English, and in essays written for this book they describe some of the difficulties they've encountered living in a new country.

Learning to speak, read, and write English is often cited as a basic problem, and one person notes that learning a new language "could be difficult when you are old." But "if you are young, you can understand" easier and more quickly.

Other common concerns include not having any friends, knowing the school rules or where classes are held, being able to figure out where to buy books, how to use the bus system, or where to find a mosque. One student writes that when he came to the United States he was upset because there was no mosque nearby where he and other Muslims could pray.

Nearly all the students complain about Minnesota's cold weather during the fall and winter. As one student puts it, "I am very fed up with the weather here. [In] Somalia every day is sunny and warm." Others were dismayed and amazed when snow fell. "I never saw a snow before," one student writes. "The first day of the snow, I was going to school and I was wearing open shoes. I was going to the bus. I was falling down." The writer, like other Somalians, had to buy new shoes for the winter months. As their teacher Jennifer Henderson notes, students found it difficult to get used to "rather large and heavy shoes," because in "Somalia they had only worn light-weight sandals due to the climate." Students told her "it was funny learning to walk in the new American shoes."[12]

In her book *The Middle of Everywhere: The World's Refugees Come to Our Town,* Mary Pipher writes about the refugee influx in Lincoln, Nebraska. Pipher was born in Nebraska (often described humorously as the "middle of nowhere"), and calls her home state a place filled with "large, rather plain, white people," including her own family.[13] Now, however, more than fifty diverse nationalities mix with the "plain, white" folks. Newcomers speak more than thirty languages, ranging from Arabic to Urdu.

Both new arrivals and native Nebraskans struggle with language barriers, often expressing frustration as they try to understand one another. Pipher stresses, though, that equally problematic for refugees is dealing for the first time with such everyday tasks as using a telephone, handling money, buying groceries, wearing Western clothing, and taking a bus. Getting used to the fast pace of American life is also difficult for those who do not measure time by the clock, but rather by natural events or by however long it takes to complete a task, conversation, or activity that has priority for the moment.

Pipher has helped a number of refugee families adjust to their new life and urges other Americans to do the

WHAT'S AMERICAN?

Apple pie? **"As American as apple pie" is a common saying, but the British are credited with creating this favorite pastry.**

Baseball? **American Abner Doubleday is often credited with originating baseball in Cooperstown, New York, in 1839, although historians have found references to the organized game being played in other cities during the 1820s; in addition, references mention boys playing baseball in England during the 1700s.**

Frozen food industry? **It's American. In the late 1800s, Clarence Birdseye of New York became a naturalist for the U.S. government and was sent to the Arctic, where he saw how indigenous people used ice, wind, and temperature to preserve food. Birdseye returned to New York to set up his own frozen food packaging company. In 1930, the first quick-frozen foods were sold under the name Birdseye.**

Jeans? **The word itself originates from a European material named for sailors from Genoa, Italy. During the gold rush days of the mid-1800s in the United States, a Bavarian immigrant named Loeb (later changed to Levi) Strauss made jeans for miners who wanted tough work clothes.**

Pizza? **Some believe this popular food originated with Italians, but before them ancient Babylonians, Egyptians, and Greeks baked large, round, flat breads that they topped with oils and spices.**

Printing press? **Johann Gutenberg was a German who invented movable type in the 1400s.**

Tee shirts? **During World War I, American troops who wore heavy wool clothing saw European soldiers wearing cool, cotton tee shirts and brought the idea for this comfortable clothing back to the United States, where the shirts quickly became popular.**

Television? **Technicians and inventors in Russia, Germany, Britain, Scotland, and Japan, as well as in the United States, contributed to the development of the first televisions.**

Vietnam Veterans Memorial? **It was created by Maya Ying Lin of Chinese ancestry—her parents emigrated from China.**

same. In an interview, she told a reporter "I would like people to ask, 'Is this person [refugee] human like me?' After asking the question, they would reach the conclusion, 'Yes, we are human together.' When they do that, there is . . . a desire to reach out."[14]

READ ALL ABOUT IT!

The essays, stories, poems, and letters in *YELL-O Girls! Emerging Voices Explore Culture, Diversity, and Growing up Asian American* dramatically tell what it means to be a young woman of Asian heritage in the United States. Included in the book are contributions by writers fifteen to twenty-two years old from across the nation. They discuss topics ranging from Asian American activism to interracial friendship and dating and white boys' "Asian fetish."

Some accounts tell about the problems and conflicts growing up in two cultures. Many of the stories dramatically describe how Asian American girls feel as they try to fit into a society that perceives them as different, even strange. Stereotyping and racist labeling (the common experience of being called a "chink") are recurrent themes. In many instances, the writings show how young Asian American women accept themselves for who they are. [Vickie Nam, ed. *YELL-O Girls! Emerging Voices Explore Culture, Diversity, and Growing up Asian American* (New York: Quill/Harper-Collins, 2001).]

Prejudice and Racism Amid Diversity

We were the objects of a lot of hate, but I had no idea how powerful that hate was.

—Lesbian teenager

Certainly, "we are human together" as author Mary Pipher emphasizes. But reaching out to anyone who appears to be different from one's own group is not commonplace for many Americans, regardless of whether they respect cultural diversity. Ethnocentrism frequently gets in the way.

Throughout history, many groups of people have claimed superiority over other cultures. Ethnocentric beliefs prompted the ancient Chinese, for example, to claim they were unique among early civilizations. Anyone who did not speak their language and adopt their customs was considered a barbarian. Ancient Egyptians thought of themselves as "more human" than any foreigners they encountered. Romans who conquered the Greeks believed they were far superior to those they ruled. Most conquerors, in fact, have believed that their ways were best.

Check it out! Ethnocentrism is a belief that one's own group is better than another.

From the 1400s through the 1600s, European explorers and conquerors returned from other continents with their ethnocentric views in tact. They had low regard for people whose skin color, customs, languages, and clothing styles differed from that of northern Europeans. Frequently, European explorers called indigenous people wherever they lived "savages" or "subhumans."

Ethnocentrism remained strong among the early European colonists in the "New World." The vast majority wanted to maintain the way of life they had known in their homelands and did not encourage diversity. In other words, it was "my way or the highway," as modern jargon might phrase it.

Is ethnocentrism a factor today in a multicultural nation like the United States? It's not necessarily called that, but certainly ethnocentric ideas are the basis for prejudice, discrimination, racism, and religious bigotry. Xenophobia—the fear of strangers or foreigners—also plays a role.

PREJUDICE

Prejudice literally means judging beforehand without knowledge or examination of the facts. Every day people prejudge one another by age, weight, hairstyle, clothes, occupation, income, religion, social status, housing, and countless other factors. Most of these prejudgments stem from negative stereotypes about individuals or groups.

Consider a complaint aired by Brad, a teenager from Colorado, who describes an experience shared by many young people on shopping trips, "A bunch of us went into this video store the other day. We were just going to rent a movie. But this old guy who owns the place kept glaring at us and started following us around. We got pissed and left. What is it about old people? Do they think all kids steal or what?"[1]

Young people with disabilities or physical differences can relate to an Illinois woman who explains what it was like when she went to a new high school, "I thought I was prepared. I know that other people think I'm strange, with my short arms and legs, but I've learned to accept my 'problem.' It's called achondroplasia—or dwarfism. Over the years I've gotten used to nicknames like Shrimp and Small Fry, but this boy really threw me. He came up to me in the hall and asked, 'When you going to join the circus?' I was upset all day. Just because I'm different doesn't mean I'm a freak!"[2]

When an Indiana woman was in her teenage years, she and her sister endured constant teasing. Why? "Because when my younger sister went to school with me, I always held her hand so the kids called us 'lezzies.' It hurt because my sister is blind, and sometimes she needed my help."[3]

Kristen, a teenager in Cumberland, Rhode Island, describes how she was the target of prejudicial behavior after she had surgery for scoliosis (curvature of the spine). She had to wear a brace, which, she writes,

> *brought many agonizing moments. I learned firsthand the cruelty of my peers. I needed to use the elevator and have my books carried. I remember having few friends those first months, yet everyone noticed me. I was known as "Brace Girl" and was constantly badgered with questions like: "Is that a bulletproof vest?" "Why do you wear that?" I got to the point that when someone even cast a questioning glance in my direction I would immediately rattle off, "It's a brace, I had surgery for scoliosis."*

Although a federal law bans discrimination in the sale or rental of houses and apartments, many real estate agents and landlords still find ways to turn away people who appear different from themselves. Photo by the author.

WHAT DO YOU THINK?

In the spring of 2001, Nicole Youngblood was not allowed to have her picture printed along with the rest of her classmates in the Tampa, Florida, Robinson High School Yearbook. Why? Because all seniors are required by school policy to follow a dress code when having their photographs taken. Male students must wear a white shirt, tie, and dark jacket. Females must wear a scooped-neck drape. Nicole refused to put on the drape. As a lesbian, she has consistently worn male-type clothing and wanted to wear a shirt, tie, and jacket. But the studio, which has a contract with the Tampa school, said Nicole needed a note from school officials stating she could be exempted from the policy. Officials said no. However, as a compromise Nicole could pay for her own picture and place it in the advertising section at the back of the yearbook.

Nicole and her mother, Sonia, would not compromise, and in June 2002 the Youngbloods sued the school, claiming that the clothing requirements for formal yearbook photographs were discriminatory and that Nicole had suffered harassment from other students and thus did not graduate until December 2001. The suit also claimed Nicole's constitutional rights had been infringed.[5]

Who was right—the school or Nicole? What do you think?

After her brace was removed, Kristen reports that she gained "tons of friends," but was saddened that many of her classmates "didn't even try to get to know me when I had my brace." Yet, she writes, "Because of my experience, now I try to include everyone and reach out to others no matter what they look like."[4]

SEXUAL PREJUDICE

Prejudice and discrimination against people because of their sexual orientation has a long history in America. In colonial times, "anyone convicted of committing a homosexual act could be sentenced to death," according to Jim Carnes.[6]

Over the years, sexual prejudice has prompted numerous assaults against gay, lesbian, bisexual, and transgendered people. The attacks usually begin with name calling, "Fag!" "Pervert!" "Dyke!" Some victims have been punched, kicked, stabbed, beaten senseless, or murdered just because they happened to be homosexual. In 1984, Charlie Howard, a homosexual living in Bangor, Maine, was beaten by three teenagers and thrown over a bridge to drown in Kenduskeag Stream. Charlie was twenty-three years old. The teenagers who attacked Charlie were arrested, convicted of murder, and sent to a youth detention center.

Another murder was committed in 1992 when Allen Schindler, a U.S. Navy enlisted man, was stomped to death in a men's room by two crewmates. In 1998, twenty-one-year-old Matthew Shepard of Casper, Wyoming, was beaten, tied to a fence, and left to die. In 2001, two Wichita, Kansas, teenagers severely beat fifty-eight-year-old Maxwell Eads, then set Eads' home on fire, which resulted in his death from burns and smoke inhalation. The motive for these murders were all the same: the men were killed because they were gay or were assumed to be homosexual.

Some people with a deep-seated prejudice against or hatred for homosexuals take pride in "gay bashing" incidents, often justifying their actions because they believe homosexual behavior is morally wrong or socially unacceptable. Or they believe homosexuality is contagious and that older homosexuals "corrupt" young people and force them to become gay or lesbian.

Polls show that nearly 50 percent of Americans generally support such beliefs, which is reflected in bans against homosexuals in the military and in laws that forbid same-sex marriages. In addition, homosexuals may be barred from some jobs and housing, even though civil rights laws provide protection against discrimination on the basis of sexual orientation.

HARASSMENT AND ATTACKS AT SCHOOLS

School campuses often are sites for harassment, physical attacks, and discrimination against homosexuals. Administrators, teachers, and other school personnel may reinforce sexual prejudice by ignoring students who taunt classmates with comments such as "you walk like a fag" or "you act so gay." Some school personnel reveal their own sexual prejudices with snide remarks, jokes, and intolerant statements about homosexuals. Coaches, for example, are known for goading male athletes with comments such as "you hit like a fag."

In Florida, a teacher told a student, Jessica Doerzapf, that she was going to hell because she was gay. A few years later, at the age of sixteen, Jessica moved to Santa Barbara, California, where she enrolled in a more tolerant school. But she still had to deal with name-calling and other verbal harassment. "I know a lot of [homosexual] people are afraid to come out because of stuff like that," Jessica told a reporter.[7]

Lesbian and gay youth are at high risk for violent attacks at school. One typical example is "a very scary incident" described by a Marion, Illinois, teenager. She explains that students and teachers at her school knew that she and her girlfriend were lesbians, thus "[w]e were the objects of a lot of hate, but I had no idea how powerful that hate was." Then one day:

> *My girlfriend, two guy friends, and I were . . . walking to our cars to go home. The two guys we were with also happened to be gay. . . . We were just about at the parking lot when all of a sudden five or six guys surrounded us and began to hit us. . . . We tried to fight back in the beginning, without success, then we just tried to huddle together to protect each other. . . . I don't think there has ever been a time when I was more afraid; I was truly afraid for my life. Those kids who beat us never got into any trouble, even though there were many people around when it happened. No one tried to stop them. It was considered okay because we were gay.*[8]

ABOUT RACE AND RACISM

Since the beginning of civilization, people within a common culture have divided themselves, but not necessarily by skin color. Ancient Greeks and Romans, for example, made distinctions between those who were civilized and those who were called barbarians. In an interview for *Atlantic Unbound,* Steve Olson, the author of *Mapping Human History,* points out that

> *a person of any skin color could be accepted into Hellenistic or Roman society so long as that person spoke the language and accepted the cultural norms of the group. A person looking exactly like a Greek or Roman who did not speak the language and was not part of the*

culture was outside of the group. The persistence of racial thinking has been particularly strong in the New World in general, and in the United States in particular, because of the unusual history of this part of the world. Groups of people with especially different appearances from very different regions were put together and subjected to powerful social forces that led to rigid social hierarchies. So people had many reasons for dividing the occupants of the New World into groups; they had biological ways of justifying those reasons; and they have relied extensively on those reasons ever since.[9]

WHAT IS RACE?

There is no universal agreement on what "race" means, and racial classification systems have varied considerably over the years. Every system has been devised by a person or persons with a particular point of view or agenda.

During the 1700s, for example, Europe had gained economic and political power, so this power along with ethnocentric beliefs prompted European biologists to categorize people by gradations of color. Caucasians, or light-skinned Europeans, got the top ranking, with Asians and indigenous Americans following, and Africans at the bottom. This system supported the myth that whites were inherently "superior," while nonwhite groups were born "innately inferior."

Other theories have been developed over the years in an attempt to categorize people by biological differences. But as J. Craig Venter, the director of the Celera Geonomics Corporation in Rockville, Maryland, notes "[r]ace is a social concept, not a scientific one. We all evolved in the last 100,000 years from the same small number of tribes that migrated out of Africa and colonized the world." According to a report in the *New York Times,* after Venter and other scientists put together the sequence of the human genome in 2000, they

unanimously declared [that] there is only one race—the human race. Dr. Venter and other researchers say that those traits most commonly used to distinguish one

> *race from another, like skin and eye color, or the width of the nose, are traits controlled by a relatively few number of genes, and thus have been able to change rapidly in response to extreme environmental pressures during the short course of Homo sapiens history. And so equatorial populations evolved dark skin, presumably to protect against ultraviolet radiation, while people in northern latitudes evolved pale skin, the better to produce vitamin D from pale sunlight.*[10]

In spite of scientific findings, dividing people by racial categories is still widely accepted as a concept in the United States (as well as in other countries). And racism and racist views continue to adversely affect the lives of millions of Americans—people of color and others labeled minorities.

WHAT IS RACISM?

Some define it as prejudice based on the belief that people can be categorized and divided by race, with one race "superior" over all others. Another definition states that racism equals prejudice plus power. Put another way, racism is an established system that grants advantages and privileges based on race. "In the context of the United States, this system clearly operates to the advantage of whites and to the disadvantage of people of color," writes Beverly Daniel Tatum, a psychology professor and dean of Mount Holyoke College.[11]

Jennifer Lynn Tweedie, a young woman of American Indian heritage, has experienced racial prejudice-plus-power most of her life. She recalls a situation when her mother signed her up for school in Florida. Her mother with light skin and Jennifer with dark coloring faced a registrar who "looked down her nose at me, and asked my mother, 'Race?' My mother said, 'American Indian.' The registrar looked back down her nose at me and said, 'Oh. We've never had one of THOSE here.' I think it was the first time I ever felt embarrassed about being Indian. Before that I was just angry when someone said something about my race."[12]

To this day, Jennifer is well aware of deeply entrenched racist attitudes. She explains that she has "been called Little Pocahontas in the workplace," and in the spring of 2002 "while speaking during a staff meeting, one of my co-workers made a comment regarding me coming after my co-workers with a tomahawk. I realize he was not trying to belittle me in front of the meeting, but it did. And it nullified everything I had said up to that point."[13]

It is not unusual today for young people and adults who are part of the dominant or majority group (that is, whites) to doubt or deny that racism still exists in U.S. culture. First, white Americans seldom encounter racism on a daily basis. Second, the majority members reason that numerous civil rights laws have been passed over the past few decades to prevent discrimination on the basis of skin color, nationality, religion, gender, sexual orientation, and disabilities. Racism, however, has not gone away; instead, it is less obvious than it was in the days when laws segregated people by color and religion.

Today, racist acts may be more subtle. They might, for instance, involve slow service or poorly prepared food at a restaurant. Cierra Benton of Chicago describes an episode that is familiar to many people of color. "Once some friends and I went to a pizza place. We were the only black people in there," she explains. "We waited about an hour and a half to order, and when our food finally came it wasn't done right."[14] Everyone else in the restaurant, however, had no problems with their order or food.

Another example comes from Indiana. A high school junior, who was the only African American on a cross-country team, tried to get along with everyone and make friends. But, as this anonymous student writes, "As the season went on . . . I started to feel out of place, like an outsider." Then after a meet one day, team members "started discussing how teens sometimes do crazy things. Then all of a sudden the issue of black and white surfaced and someone said, 'Whites are superior to blacks, blacks have issues.' The saddest part of this was realizing they knew I was there and didn't care. My world crumbled as they made comment after comment and laughed. Reality smacked me in the face. I'd had my first encounter with discrimination."[15]

WHAT KEEPS PREJUDICE AND RACISM ALIVE?

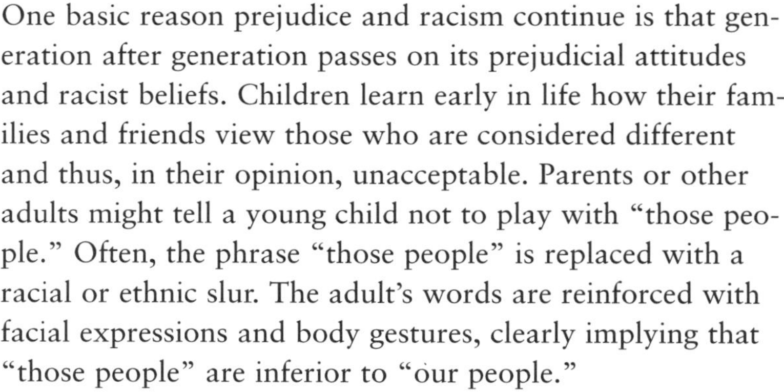

One basic reason prejudice and racism continue is that generation after generation passes on its prejudicial attitudes and racist beliefs. Children learn early in life how their families and friends view those who are considered different and thus, in their opinion, unacceptable. Parents or other adults might tell a young child not to play with "those people." Often, the phrase "those people" is replaced with a racial or ethnic slur. The adult's words are reinforced with facial expressions and body gestures, clearly implying that "those people" are inferior to "our people."

Even if young people do not absorb prejudices at home, they may learn as they go through school, attend social events, and watch television shows or movies that it's okay to put down people who appear different from themselves. Schools, for example, often are sites for cultural conflicts and prejudicial behavior.

Consider just one incident that took place in 2001 at Edison High School in Huntington Beach, California. During a current events discussion on immigration, some students began to belittle Mexican immigrants, calling them "wetbacks" and insisting that Mexicans were trying to take over the United States. Lizdebeth Villasenor, the only student of Mexican heritage in the class, tried to speak up and counter the statements, but, as she told a newspaper reporter, "nobody heard me because I sit way in the back."[16] That same day, Lizdebeth's sister, Veronica, a junior in the same school, was subjected to similar remarks when a student recounted what had been discussed in Lizdebeth's class.

Understandably, the two teenagers were extremely upset and hurt, but Lizdebeth did not remain silent. She decided to take action and reported the incident to the school principal. He, in turn, demanded that the student who had made most of the prejudicial remarks apologize to both Lizdebeth and Veronica.

STEREOTYPES OF MIGRANT WORKERS

American citizens of Mexican heritage who happen to be migrant farmworkers face frequent discrimination and exploitation and some of the most consistent stereotyping. Between three and five million people travel from the West and East Coasts and throughout the midsection of the United States, following the planting and harvesting cycles in North America. They support a multibillion-dollar agricultural industry in the United States.

Some migrant families—including young children and teenagers—have planted and picked crops for several generations, but they have long been viewed as illegal immigrants looking for a handout and not to be trusted. Seldom are they seen as hardworking people trying to eke out a living. Cynthia, a teenage migrant worker who was born in Mission, Texas, travels with her family—her parents, two sisters, and a brother—from Texas to Pasco, Washington, each year. She writes:

> *My father has been bringing people to work in the asparagus as a crew leader. I, as a migrant, help my dad work in the fields on weekends. . . . I think working in the fields is very hard, because you need to work in the sun all day. . . . My parents get to keep most of the money I earn, so they can pay the bills they owe, or pay other things they need to pay. My parents give me some amount of money, so that I can buy clothes for the following year of school. . . . What I like least about being a migrant worker is to change from school to school in different places.*[17]

Wherever they work, migrant laborers are among the lowest paid in the U.S. labor force, earning annual incomes below the federal poverty level. Besides poor pay, farmworkers face health hazards from unsanitary working conditions and exposure to toxic pesticides while planting or harvesting in the fields. Federal regulations require that workers stay out of a field for a specific length of time after pesticide spraying, but those rules are not always followed or workers are not warned about the dangers. Each year, tens of thousands of migrant farmworkers suffer illnesses due to pesticide exposure.[18] No one knows the exact number of poisonings because victims seldom seek medical care; they are not likely to have health insurance coverage and are reluctant to miss work. Migrant health centers, where available, do provide care, but they serve fewer than 20 percent of the nation's farmworkers. If farmworkers get to a health center, doctors may fail to diagnose accurately because poisoning symptoms are similar to those associated with the flu.

Migrant laborers often work without adequate toilets, drinking water, and hand-washing facilities in the fields, which leads to other health hazards. When workers do not have sufficient drinking water, they become dehydrated or suffer from other heat-related problems. Lack of water for hand washing leads to the spread of communicable diseases and allows pesticide residues to remain on their skin.

For the past few years, Frank Gillen, a Tampa University professor, has required his students in his freshman English course to write research papers on migrant labor. Students must see firsthand how field laborers work and live by going to the field, talking to workers, and listening to laborers who visit the class. One student reports, "I have learned about people who have it worse than me. . . . My problems just don't seem as big anymore. I never knew how bad farmworkers' lifestyles are. I never even took a second glance at them. Being able to meet some workers, see their homes and hear their voices are images I'll never forget."[19]

Some U.S. citizens of Mexican heritage are migrant workers who travel from South to North to plant and harvest crops. They not only are stereotyped, but often have to live and work under primitive conditions for inadequate pay. Photos courtesy of the Farm Labor Research Project, Toledo, Ohio.

"WHITE PRIVILEGE"

Many Americans who are part of the majority white population seldom are aware of the advantages and privileges that they enjoy, which sometimes prevents them from seeing or empathizing with the way prejudicial attitudes and racism are institutionalized—ingrained in social, economic, educational, religious, law enforcement, and other systems in U.S. society. Of course, not all whites are overtly racist, but the advantage system (or the white privilege system, as it's been called) helps perpetuate racism. A journalism professor at the University of Texas explains how he, as a Caucasian, has enjoyed white privileges:

> *Rather than try to tell others how white privilege has played out in their lives, I talk about how it has affected me. I am as white as white gets in this country. I am of northern European heritage and I was raised in North Dakota, one of the whitest states in the country. I grew up in a virtually all-white world surrounded by racism, both personal and institutional. Because I didn't live near a reservation, I didn't even have exposure to the state's only numerically significant non-white population, American Indians.*
>
> *I have struggled to resist that racist training and the ongoing racism of my culture. I like to think I have changed, even though I routinely trip over the lingering effects of that internalized racism and the institutional racism around me. But no matter how much I "fix" myself, one thing never changes—I walk through the world with white privilege.*
>
> *What does that mean? Perhaps most importantly when I seek admission to a university, apply for a job, or hunt for an apartment, I don't look threatening. Almost all of the people evaluating me look like me—they are white. They see in me a reflection of themselves—and in a racist world, that is an advantage. . . . I am one of them. I am not dangerous. Even when I voice critical opinions, I am cut some slack.*[20]

SCAPEGOATS FOR ECONOMIC PROBLEMS

Check it out!
Caucasian is a term used to describe white or light-skinned people. The name came from the Caucasus mountain range between Russia and Georgia and was coined in 1795 by Johann Friedrich Blumenach, who was greatly impressed by the people of the Caucasus region and concluded they probably were the first humans created.

Another factor that contributes to ongoing prejudice and racism is a declining economy. Some Americans tend to blame joblessness and financial hardships on the most convenient scapegoats. Those scapegoats frequently are immigrants, who are accused of taking jobs that would otherwise be offered to U.S. citizens. Those jobs, however, are usually low paying and in occupations noted for poor working conditions, such as meat packing, poultry processing, farm labor, and the garment industry.

Many workers in U.S. poultry processing plants, for example, are recent immigrants—about half of the total 245,000 workers in the industry. Some immigrants take the jobs because they offer a legal means to come to the United States. A *Washington Post* report explains how Korean middle-class families pay up to $30,000 to work at poultry processing plants in Maryland:

> *Immigration brokers advertise the poultry jobs in Korean newspapers as a shortcut to the United States. Koreans who respond pay $10,000 to $30,000 in fees and promise to work for a year in processing plants. . . . When they are hired, they receive legal permanent U.S. residency for themselves and their families under a federal program designed to fill unskilled jobs. For some, the process shortens a possible fifteen-year wait to immigrate. For others, it is the only legal means of coming to America.*
>
> *Under the program, U.S. companies can import foreign workers once they prove to the Labor Department that they have advertised and recruited extensively yet still have openings.*[21]

Guatemalan and Mexican immigrants also fill many jobs in poultry processing plants as do many blacks. Still, there is constant turnover in this industry and jobs are readily available—if Americans want to apply for them.

Numerous other factors can perpetuate racism and prejudice, from lack of enforcement of civil rights legislation to groups that denounce those who do not share their religious beliefs. In addition, words and images in a great variety of media play a significant role in how Americans of diverse cultures are perceived.

4 Racist Images and Stereotypes

Why can't we let everyone know that biracial people are just like people of all other races? Why can't [the public] know we are normal?

—Maia Benjamin-Wardle, a person of mixed-race ancestry[1]

For decades, words and images have been powerful forces in keeping stereotypes and racism alive in the United States. Advertisements, movies, television (TV) programs, textbooks, religious sermons, political campaigns, and numerous products, such as toys, games, artifacts, packaged foods, and yard ornaments, have reflected (and still do in some cases) disparaging images of people who are not part of the majority.

Mass-produced items have often revealed the attitudes of the ruling class or dominant group. This was especially true during the late 1800s and early 1900s when toy and game manufacturers created products that depicted grotesque caricatures of black Americans and many recently arrived immigrant groups. White Americans bought and used the products because they felt there was nothing wrong with demeaning or ridiculing those they believed to be "inferior."

Although many of today's products and media feature people of diverse ethnic and racial heritages in a realistic and honest manner, stereotypes persist. People who are "dwarfed," for example, have been frequently depicted in movies as sideshow entertainers, the physically disabled as "sinister," girls and women as "frail" and "emotional," Italians as mafia types, Poles as "stupid," Irish as "drunks," and so on.

RACIST IMAGES OF NATIVE PEOPLES

Some of the most persistent racist images are those of Native peoples. Who hasn't seen cartoons or "Wild West" films showing cowboys and warlike American Indians? Or watched (or played) some version of a cowboy-and-Indian game complete with the whoops and hollering of stereotyped

"YOU CAN QUOTE ME"

Children Now **interviewed Native American youth in 1999, asking young people what the public learns about Native Americans from watching TV dramas. The answers, "They're poor," "All drunk," "They live on reservations," "Dance around fires and stuff," and "They all drive pick-up trucks." Asked what their ideal show would be like, a Seattle teenager offered the following advice, "If they're going to put Indians [in a show], I'd tell them to actually go and study what they're about to film."[2]**

war cries. Who hasn't seen various media portrayals of so-called American Indian villages with tipis? Or American Indian caricatures with feathered headdresses? Who hasn't heard the rasping greeting "how" or "ugh" accompanied by a raised hand, a white-created, false concept of American Indian behavior? Or heard a female of Native American heritage referred to by the offensive term "squaw" (equivalent to "whore" or female genitalia), or a male hailed as "chief" or "Crazy Horse," essentially denying a person's name and tribal affiliation, and thereby dismissing his or her identity?

From the time children learn the English alphabet, they are frequently taught through blocks, coloring books, puzzles, and other graphic materials that the letter "I" stands for Indian—a caricature wearing a headband with a feather or a full-feather headdress. This is not a representation of all Native peoples and the image has nothing to do with present-day tribal life. "I isn't for Indian . . . it is often for Ignorance. In the Never-Never Land of glib stereotypes and caricature, the rich histories, cultures, and contemporary complexities of the indigenous, diverse peoples of the Western Hemisphere are obscured, misrepresented, and rendered trivial," writes Michael A. Dorris in the foreword to the first edition of *American Indian Stereotypes in the World of Children.*[3] As this volume documents, stereotypes of American Indians are commonplace in the United States. Toys, storybooks, textbooks (including history texts), advertisements, films, pageants, and countless items such as plaques, tee shirts, caps, mugs, and numerous souvenirs carry demeaning messages about the cultures of Native peoples.

Some examples of toys that stereotype indigenous people. Photo by John Goodwin.

These put-downs have persisted ever since European explorers set foot on the hemisphere that was eventually named for Amerigo Vespucci, an Italian navigator. In written accounts and in visuals, Indians (named by explorers who thought they were in India) have been presented as "warlike," "uncivilized," "heathens," "drunks," and people "living off the government." Such stereotypes frequently ignore the fact that the federal governments of both the United States and Canada have been responsible for the loss of Native lands, placing Native Americans on reservations, isolating them from the rest of society, and forcing dependency.

Some stereotypes of Native peoples if not outright insults are romanticized images of American Indian life. Jennifer Lynn Tweedie, who has a Native American heritage, notes, "Every time a Native American person is on television, movies, etc. the mystical music comes on, and there is always something very spiritual happening. People don't understand that we also just hang out, go to the grocery store and tie our shoes just like everyone else."[4]

When outdoor dramas and pageants include characters of Native heritage, cast members frequently dress in costumes that have little or no association with the indigenous people they are attempting to represent. Photo by Douglas Gay.

INSULTING INDIAN ICONS

Some of the most insulting, racist images of indigenous peoples appear at sporting events at high schools, colleges, and professional arenas. Many non-Native people see no harm in using warriorlike Indian images and actually believe that they honor American Indians by using a tribal name for a sports team or a generic name such as "Braves," "Chiefs," or "Redskins," a term coined by early colonists who received bounties for the capture of American Indians' red skins. Cornel Pewewardy, a University of Kansas professor with Comanche-Kiowa heritage, notes, "Indigenous Peoples would never have associated the sacred practices of becoming a warrior with the hoopla of a pep rally, half-time entertainment, or a side-kick to cheerleaders . . . making fun of Indigenous Peoples in athletic events across the country is wrong!" In addition, Pewewardy points out, "As long as such negative mascots and logos remain within the arena of

"CHASCO FIASCO"

Today, the U.S. government recognizes well over five hundred Indian tribes. Yet, most non-Natives have little or no understanding of the diverse groups and accept without question the false and racist portrayals of indigenous peoples. For example, in New Port Richey, Florida, a group of young people took part in a pageant that until 2003 was presented annually in conjunction with the Chasco Fiesta. The pageant is based on a Chasco history written in 1922 by Gerben M. DeVries, a white man and local postmaster. Performed by non-Native young people, the play referred to indigenous people as heathens, acting out a legend based on the idea that the great white fathers and mothers and their religion are superior to any others and should be all powerful. The pageant was finally discontinued after numerous protests by the American Indian Movement (AIM).

However, the fiesta itself continues. According to the fiesta's website, "Since 1922, Chasco Fiesta has honored the romantic legend intertwining the lives of a Spanish boy and girl, a priest and the Calusa Indian tribe who captured them after defeating a Spanish expedition."[5] But members of AIM's Florida chapter do not believe they and their heritage are being honored as the festival organizers claim.

Since 1995, AIM members have staged peaceful protests against the festival theme, usually surrounded by dozens of local police, even though protestors carry only small signs and for the most part stand in silence. Festival organizers have not been swayed and have made no move to change their practices, contending that the fiesta is a longstanding tradition. But "so was slavery," notes Ruby Beaulieu, AIM's Pasco County director. "Non-Natives dressing up like Indians and trying to act the way they think Native peoples behave is offensive. It hurts," Beaulieu says.[6]

Sheridan Murphy, the Florida executive director of AIM, wants to see "the racist Chasco Fiasco" eliminated or revamped so that Native peoples are not exploited and demeaned.[7] The National Congress of American Indians (NCAI) of the United States supports this view and endorses the work of Native American groups who are attempting to educate "the Florida non-Indian community, regarding the concept of racial exploitation, religious violation, spiritual violation, cultural exploitation and psychological harm" that are the result of the "use of American Indians as a mock festival known as the Chasco Indian Festival." In a resolution adopted in February 2002, the NCAI also stated that it supports educating the community regarding the stereotypes perpetuated by "non-Indian peoples dressing up in 'feathers and buckskin' type clothing, allowing their children to use the 'tomahawk chop,' and using the 'woo woo' sound, even conducting a parade of such behavior, including an Indian Princess contest, being performed primarily by the non-Indian community who unknowingly generate harm against Native peoples families and Native children."[8]

school activities, both Indigenous and non-Indigenous" young people will learn or continue to believe that it's okay to tolerate racism.[9]

Today, no other racial group is stereotyped at sporting events. Imagine, for example, mocking African Americans with a white person in blackface as a mascot, or using a grinning Latino character in a sombrero as a logo, or naming a team Chinks. A sports stadium would erupt with angry denunciations. Yet, an estimated two thousand U.S. schools use American Indian tribal names for their sports teams, because students and officials associate the name with the false stereotype of an aggressive, warlike people. Usually, the team events include mascots or logos on clothing and equipment that depict cartoon American Indian images—some of them extremely offensive.

Because of protests and education efforts, many high schools have begun to eliminate images that are caricatures of Native peoples. Yet, in some cases getting rid of stereotypical clownlike Indian images is difficult. Non–American Indian students may be unaware of the harm that these demeaning images inflict on Native peoples, alumni may insist that school traditions must be maintained, and school officials and teachers may think that using an American Indian image is a nonissue.

In April 2001, the U.S. Commission on Civil Rights urged school districts and colleges to end the use of American Indian names and mascots at non–American Indian schools. According to a report in the *San Francisco Chronicle,* the commission wrote, "Schools have a responsibility to educate their students. They should not use their influence to perpetuate misrepresentations of any culture or people."[10]

BLACK STEREOTYPES

Since the days of slavery, negative images of African Americans have been widely circulated in the United States. One of the most degrading is the black male as a buffoon, represented by Sambo, Rastus, Uncle Remus, Stepin Fetchit, and other characters. A grotesque form of the caricature has oversized bright red lips, bulging eyes, and very dark skin. He is always grinning broadly, dancing, singing, joking—or being the butt of jokes—eating watermelon, and looking and acting foolish for the entertainment of white folks. Most of these representations stemmed from slavery—a time when black men, women, and children were expected to sing and dance as well as work for their "masters."

After emancipation, the male black stereotype and his female counterpart, often known as "Mammy" or "Aunt Jemima," appeared in numerous formats—from advertisements, to product and restaurant names, to stage presentations. From the 1920s through the 1950s, demeaning stereotypes of black Americans appeared on countless artifacts and products. White Americans thought nothing of buying and using such items as a cookie jar shaped in the form of a heavyset black woman, wearing a kerchief and white apron, or placing a blackfaced iron jockey on a lawn.

Such institutionalized images kept alive the myth that blacks were second rate or less than human. These images were frequently accompanied by such put-down labels as "darkey," "pickaninny," and "coon." The latter term along with "nigger" is one of the most insulting labels.

"The name itself, an abbreviation of raccoon, is dehumanizing," writes David Pilgrim, a professor of sociology at Ferris State University in Michigan. "As with Sambo, the coon was portrayed as a lazy, easily frightened, chronically idle, inarticulate buffoon. The coon differed from the Sambo [character] in subtle but important ways. Sambo was depicted as a perpetual child, not capable of living as an independent adult. The coon acted childish, but he was an adult; albeit a good-for-little adult."[11]

Pilgrim has collected four thousand artifacts that depict these racist images, from sheet music to salt and pepper shakers, which are displayed at the Jim Crow Museum of Racist Memorabilia at Ferris State University in Big Rapids, Michigan. The museum was named for a "minstrel show character created by Thomas Dartmouth Rice in the early

1830s . . . a white actor who blackened his face with burnt cork and performed a song-and-dance act said to have been inspired by an elderly black man from the South. Rice's tattered costume and exaggerated movements and voice were an insulting parody that brought him international acclaim."[12]

Why would anyone establish such a museum? Founder and curator Pilgrim explains that as a teenager he saw these artifacts at flea markets and garage sales. They "would offend me, and I'd buy them to destroy them. I got older and recognized the historical significance of these items. I stopped destroying them and started collecting them." Now, in the museum, the memorabilia are part of his effort to promote a scholarly examination of racism. The items "force a person to take a stand for or against the equality of all human beings." For example, one especially despicable item is a framed picture of black children sitting on a sand bar. Under the image is the caption, "Alligator Bait."

Pilgrim points out that most of the artifacts were ordinary household objects used by "average citizens," not necessarily militant racists such as Ku Klux Klan members. Some are antiques but others were manufactured in recent years. "There is a really strong market for these items right now," says Pilgrim, "and the more racist the item, the more it costs. At this point, the museum is not a true sample of what's out there. It's a sample of what I could afford. A lot of these items are in peoples' homes today."[13]

Underscoring this point, an alligator cookie jar is just one modern-day item that has a racist bent. Offered on a dozen websites, it is advertised as a talking alligator that says, "Mm . . . Mmm . . . Those are some tasty cookies." However, when the jar is opened it actually says, "Mmm-mmm. Those sho' is some tasty cookies." This present-day object uses a stereotyped black dialect, and, whether intended or not, it also associates alligators with the false concept that the animals are by nature attracted to blacks, the basis for numerous racist jokes on the topic.

A talking alligator cookie jar that "speaks" in stereotyped black dialect. Photo by the author.

IN AND OUT OF THE PICTURE

What about depictions of black Americans in other media? African Americans seldom appeared on film in the early 1900s and one of the first TV shows to feature a black cast was *Amos 'n' Andy* in 1951. The TV version was a carry-over from a widely popular radio show that began in 1928 and featured white characters speaking in dialect.

Debates over *Amos 'n' Andy* are long-standing. While many praise the comedic script and acting, the show has also been labeled as racist. "Every character in this one and only TV show with an all Negro cast is either a clown or a crook," as the National Association for the Advancement of Colored People (NAACP) noted in 1951. Production on the show stopped in 1953, but it was syndicated in the early 1960s and when reruns appeared, protestors voiced their complaints of racism. By 1966, *Amos 'n' Andy* had been dropped from most stations.

From the 1960s through the 1980s, TV and movies began to include black actors and actresses in supporting roles. In addition, shows featuring black comedians—*Julia, Sanford and Son, The Jeffersons,* and *The Cosby Show*—appeared. Today, black performers are featured on numerous TV shows and in popular movies. But many critics argue that real life in black America is seldom shown. Some comedic characters purposely do "shuckin and jivin" routines (suggesting the clownlike images of Jim Crow days), while other black performers may play subordinate roles—maids, butlers, gardeners, chauffeurs, cooks, and so on—or they play characters who are pimps, gang members, or others with antisocial attitudes and behaviors.

Another type of film that has been popular since the 1990s is the "buddy movie," which appears to show authentic black-white friendships (*Lethal Weapon* with Danny Glover and Mel Gibson as partner cops is just one example). While the buddy films highlight positive black characters, they give the impression that racial divisions and institutional racism no longer exist. But, like many Hollywood productions, the films are fantasy. In the real world, as one critic notes, the dominant white social order is still in place.[14]

ASIAN AMERICAN AND LATINO CARICATURES

Throughout most of U.S. history, dark-skinned Latinos and Asian Americans have been stereotyped in many of the same ways that blacks and Native peoples have been portrayed—frequently as clowns, criminals, or not-too-bright sidekicks. For example, there's the hot señorita, the Latin lover, the Mexican bandit, and the sleeping (read "lazy") Latino in a sombrero. Demeaning images of Asians include the subservient Chinese cook or laundry worker, usually shown with exaggerated slanted eyes, buck teeth, and shaved head with queue or wearing a rice paddy hat. Or there are Asian males shown as karate fighters or sinister spies.

Even in recent times caricatures prevail. For example, in April 2002 Abercrombie and Fitch (A&F) began promoting and selling so-called multicultural tee shirts that displayed offensive Asian stereotypes. Caricatures of slant-eyed Asians in conical hats carried the slogan "Wong Brothers Laundry Service: Two Wongs Can Make it White." Another shirt portrayed a man pulling a rickshaw with the phrase "Rick Shaw's Hoagies and Grinders. Order by the foot. Good meat. Quick feet." Still another said "Wok-N-Bowl, Let the Good Times Roll, Chinese Food & Bowling."

Check it out!

Among Asian Americans are people with diverse ancestry: Chinese, Japanese, Korean, Cambodian, Laotian, Hmong, Vietnamese, Taiwanese, some Arabs and Indians (from India), and Pacific Islanders. Latinos/Latinas (referred to as Hispanics in U.S. census data) are Spanish speaking and include people of Mexican, Puerto Rican, Cuban, and Central and South American heritage. Some Latinos/Latinas may also be labeled or consider themselves to be black Americans or Native peoples.

Spontaneous protests erupted in numerous cities across the United States. One protest forced a new A&F store to delay its grand opening. Chinese American groups demanded not only an apology, but also urged that A&F employees receive diversity training and that potential customers boycott the stores. The company pulled the shirts from its store shelves and website, but insisted that the racist images were simply a humorous attempt—a spoof—to appeal to the growing Asian market.

MORE NEGATIVE STEREOTYPES

Another negative stereotype that has had a long life in the American culture is the Jewish caricature, presented in numerous forms. In cartoons, film, and other media, Jewish caricatures have been shown or described as "Christ killers," "tightwads," and "swindlers."

Historically, stereotypes of Jews have been based on the false belief that Jews were responsible for the death of Jesus. In addition, there has been a long-held resentment of Jewish immigrants in America who managed to rise from rags to riches. Usually, these monetary rewards were the result of menial labor, pushcart sales, and careful money management. Such efforts have been labeled "pushiness" and "greed" when applied to Jews, but are called "hard work" and "thrift" when related to other immigrant groups.

Although the number of people with stereotyped views of Jews declined in the United States during the 1990s, a national survey in 2002 by the Anti-Defamation League (ADL) finds that 17 percent of Americans hold strong anti-Semitic beliefs, an increase of 5 percent from a survey taken in 1998. Anti-Semitism is particularly strong among Latinos/Hispanics, with 35 percent of those surveyed expressing negative opinions about Jews. The same percentage of African Americans also expressed such views. Abraham H. Foxman, the ADL national director, notes that "[w]hile there are many factors at play, all of the evidence suggests that a strong undercurrent of Jewish hatred persists in America." The ADL survey finds that anti-Israel feelings are triggering anti-Semitism. "Negative attitudes toward Israel and concern that American Jews have too much influence over U.S. Middle East policy are helping to foster anti-Semitic beliefs," the survey notes.[15]

The Middle East conflicts (as well as the September 11, 2001, terrorist attacks) have also brought to the forefront negative images of Arabs and Muslims. Stereotypes of Arabs are not new, however. For decades, cartoons, comic strips, illustrations in children's books, and even Halloween costumes have presented Arabs in an unfavorable manner. Such comic strips as *Annie, Brenda Starr, Broom Hilda,* and *The Wizard of Id* have portrayed Arabs with unflattering facial features and have characterized Arabs as "arrogant, rich oil sheiks," "shifty, menacing villains," "crooked and greedy," or as "terrorists." These stereotypes of Arabs have become even more widespread in the United States since the terrorist attacks, and Arab Americans have become targets

Although this photo was taken in 1986, when Arab Americans were protesting an NBC documentary *Under Siege*, which stereotyped people of Arab ancestry, this scene depicts the way many Arab Americans feel today—under siege. Photo courtesy of the American-Arab Anti-Discrimination Committee.

for harassment and violent acts. Frequently, they are targets because in many parts of the United States Arab culture and Arab Americans are misunderstood.

In 2001, the *Detroit (Michigan) Free Press* and the Knight Ridder news syndicate published a journalists' guide to answer questions about Arab Americans, many of whom live in Michigan. "There are no easy, one-size-fits-all answers," the handbook states. "Culture, language and religion are distinct qualities that act in different ways to connect Arabs, and to distinguish them from one another." In response to a question about ancestry, the guide notes, "Arab Americans trace their roots to many places, including parts or all of Algeria, Bahrain, Djibouti, Egypt, Iraq, Jordan, Kuwait, Lebanon, Libya, Mauritania, Morocco, Oman, Palestine, Qatar, Saudi Arabia, Somalia, Sudan, Syria, Tunisia, United Arab Emirates and Yemen. Some Arabs are Israeli citizens."[16]

Perhaps one of the most widespread misconceptions is the religious affiliation of Arab Americans. Contrary to popular belief, most Arab Americans are not Muslims or followers of Islam. They "belong to many religions, including Islam, Christianity, Druze, Judaism and others. There are further distinctions within each of these, and some religious groups have evolved new identities and faith practices in the United States. . . . Most Arab Americans are Catholic or Orthodox Christians, but this is not true in all parts of the United States," where the majority may be Muslim.[17]

Muslims and the Islamic faith are frequently tied to terrorism by those who believe stereotypes and accept negative images of various groups of Americans. In fact, religious bigotry is one of the most tenacious forms of prejudice and is common in most countries of the world. The United States is no exception, even though it is a nation that proclaims all people should have the right to worship according to their beliefs.

5 Religious Diversity and Conflicts

What frightens me is people fighting so violently over religion, in the name of trying to convince others. Religion should be about love.

—Seventeen-year-old Jamaul[1]

Religious conflicts have been common since colonial days in America. While some of the early colonists hoped to find religious liberty, that does not mean that they supported religious freedom for everyone. With the exception of Rhode Island, Pennsylvania, and Delaware, each colony set up a state church and expected all settlers to abide by its doctrine. Virginia founders, for example, established the Anglican Church patterned after the Church of England. Virginia laws required everyone to attend church, and those who did not accept church teachings were harshly punished.

In the Massachusetts Bay Colony, founded by British religious dissenters known as Puritans, leaders strictly enforced the rules of the Congregational Church (their established religion). Catholics and members of such Protestant groups as Baptists and Quakers were harassed, publicly beaten, and driven from the colony. In the Maryland colony, Catholics and some Protestant groups could worship as they chose. However, Unitarians, Jews, and others who denied that Jesus was the son of God risked death if they expressed such views.

THE FIRST AND FOURTEENTH AMENDMENTS

After the American Revolution, newly formed states slowly began to accept religious differences, and the First and Fourteenth Amendments to the U.S. Constitution provided for the free exercise of religion. The First Amendment begins with the sentence, "Congress shall make no law respecting an establishment of religion, or prohibiting the free exercise thereof." The first clause, often called the "establishment clause," makes it clear that Congress cannot pass a law to establish or support a state church—that is, the federal government cannot favor one religion over another. The second clause provides for the free exercise of religion. The First Amendment is backed by the Fourteenth Amendment, which declares in part that no state can "deprive any person of life, liberty, or property, without due process of law; nor deny to any person within its jurisdiction the equal protection of the laws." The Fourteenth Amendment makes clear that state governments must adhere to the Constitution's Bill of Rights just as the federal government does.

In controversies over differences in religious beliefs, the First Amendment is usually quoted and it is frequently interpreted as establishing a "wall of separation" between church and state. But over the years, numerous legal arguments have been raised over how high that wall should be or whether that wall should be more like a picket fence that allows some barriers to be removed to accommodate religious practices. In some cases, the U.S. Supreme Court has had to decide whether the establishment clause has been violated. Consider these examples from the twentieth century:

- During the 1920s, John T. Scopes, a biology teacher in Tennessee, taught the theory of evolution in his high school classes. At the time, state law prohibited teaching anything that denied the biblical story of creation. Scopes was convicted of violating the law, but his lawyer, famous attorney Clarence Darrow, threatened to take the case to the U.S. Supreme Court and the Tennessee Supreme Court eventually overturned the trial court decision.
- Until the 1940s, most states required students to salute and pledge allegiance to the U.S. flag. But Jehovah's Witnesses, some Mennonites, and a few other groups believe that the salute and pledge are against biblical law. A member of the Jehovah's Witnesses challenged the ceremony in court, and in 1943, the U.S. Supreme Court ruled that authorities could not compel anyone to recite the pledge.
- During the 1960s, Adelle Sherbert, a Seventh-Day Adventist in South Carolina, refused to work on Saturday, her religion's Sabbath. She quit her job and

applied for unemployment benefits, which the state denied. When Sherbert's case went to the Supreme Court, the justices ruled a state cannot deny a person unemployment benefits if he or she quits a job that infringes the free exercise of religion.

- In 1963, the Edward Schempp family of Germantown, Pennsylvania, sued the state because of its mandate that ten verses of the Bible should be read daily in public school classrooms. As Unitarians, the Schempps could not agree with the religious practices in the schools. The Supreme Court eventually ruled that the required Bible reading was unconstitutional.
- During the 1970s, an Amish family in Wisconsin refused to obey state laws requiring children to attend public school until the age of sixteen. The Amish traditionally are farmers and they reject most modern conveniences. They send their children to private church schools through eighth grade. After that, young people are expected to work on the farm. After the Wisconsin family refused to abide by the state's compulsory education law, their case was heard by the Supreme Court. The justices ruled in the family's favor, stating that the state law jeopardized the freedom of the family to live by their beliefs.

Over the past few decades, Americans have tolerated many more religious practices than they did in earlier times. In fact, the *U.S. News and World Report* notes that the United States has become much more religiously diverse. "Muslims, Buddhists, Hindus, Sikhs, Jains, Zoroastrians, and others have arrived in increasing numbers, dramatically altering the religious landscape of many communities. . . . Though the numbers of non-Christians are relatively small—about 6.5 percent of the U.S. population—their visibility and influence are growing. Nationwide, there are now more Buddhists than Presbyterians and nearly as many Muslims as Jews."[2]

What does this mean for Christian denominations that have long claimed a common heritage? They must increasingly take into account fellow citizens who do not share

their beliefs or who have no religious affiliations. This can lead to controversies over whose religion is the authentic one. In an anonymous article posted on iEmily.com, a health site for teenagers, a nineteen-year-old Mormon describes some of the discriminatory practices at the evangelical Christian Academy she attended. Beginning with her junior year, she was active in music, varsity softball, and drama, and became well known in the school. But, she writes,

> *[a]lmost immediately, the crusade began. If well-meaning friends weren't questioning me, or ignorant enemies weren't berating me, then I was surrounded by teachers and students who made it their personal duty to proselytize to me. In my volunteer work, the coordinator would play gospel music and preach doctrine to me between projects.*
>
> *I became frustrated by the fact that these people refused to recognize me as what I am: a Christian. I found that even though no one was completely closed-minded, more often than not, misinformation or misconception kept me from many things.*
>
> *The worst blow came at the end of my junior year. I was simultaneously running for the chorale chaplain position and auditioning for an elite choir. In both cases, my victory was almost entirely ensured. One hour before the decisions were to be announced, I was called into the principal's office and asked, on religious grounds, to withdraw from both the race for the leadership position and the choir audition. Not wanting to make matters worse, I agreed.*[3]

The writer notes that during her senior year she was subjected to similar discrimination, but her story had a positive ending. Her musical ability was recognized with the Senior Music Award; she made history as the first Mormon to receive the honor. She concludes, "I never thought, as a Caucasian female, that I'd have to deal with being a minority, but my experience has given me new appreciation for those who have to deal with it on a regular basis."[4]

BIGOTRY OR STATEMENTS OF FAITH?

Many conservative Christians (evangelicals and fundamentalists who interpret the Bible literally) consider it their duty to convert nonreligious people and those of other faiths, preaching that a person must believe in Jesus as the only road to salvation and heaven. But non-Christian groups as well as nonbelievers may resent any conversion efforts. In short, when one group decides its religious views are "right" and the others are "wrong," the stage is set for conflict.

Consider the views of Franklin Graham, the son of famed evangelist Billy Graham. An NBC news report in November 2001 quoted Graham as saying, "The God of Islam is not the same God. He's not the son of God of the Christian or Judeo-Christian faith. It's a different God, and I believe it is a very evil and wicked religion." After speaking at a dedication of a North Carolina chapel, Graham was interviewed by an NBC journalist. Graham declared, "I don't believe [Islam] is a wonderful, peaceful religion. . . . When you read the Koran and you read the verses from the Koran, it instructs the killing of the infidel, for those who are non-Muslim." He added, "It wasn't Methodists flying in to those buildings, and it wasn't Lutherans. It was an attack on this country by people of the Islamic faith."[5]

After protests from Muslim groups and interfaith organizations, Graham wrote a column for the *Wall Street Journal* to claim that he was "greatly misunderstood" and that "as a minister, not a politician, I believe it is my responsibility to speak out against the terrible deeds that are committed as a result of Islamic teaching. . . . The persecution or elimination of non-Muslims has been a cornerstone of Islamic conquests and rule for centuries. The Koran provides ample evidence that Islam encourages violence in order to win converts and to reach the ultimate goal of an Islamic world."[6]

Graham's published opinions did not appease varied religious and civil rights groups who have frequently been at odds with fundamental Christians' statements. Television evangelist Pat Robertson, for example, once called American Muslims responsible for slavery. On his *700 Club* program,

A DECLARATION

The American Baptist Churches of the USA issued a declaration in 2001 "to recognize the prevalence of stereotyping and prejudice against Islam, Muslims and Arabs and the violence associated with this bigotry. In order to help free ourselves from this racism and ethnic and religious bigotry, American Baptists are called to undertake the following:

1. **To pursue a better understanding of Islam, Muslims and Arabs (including Arab Christians) by including in their churches' educational programs a study of Islam, of the Muslim world and the Christian minorities within that world, and of the issues that have united and divided us by inviting Muslims and Arabs to be a part of the leadership and fellowship of such programs;**
2. **To encourage local and regional ecumenical and interfaith agencies to seek conversation and cooperation with Muslim religious organizations;**
3. **To advocate and defend the civil rights of Arabs and Muslims living in the United States by such means as monitoring organizations and agencies which exercise responsibility for the peace, welfare and security of the community;**
4. **To reject the religious and political demagoguery and manipulation manifest in the reporting of events related to the Middle East, to seek an understanding of the underlying causes of the events and to condemn violence as a means of enforcing national will or achieving peace;**
5. **To challenge and rebut statements made about Islam, Muslims and Arabs that embody religious stereotyping, prejudice and bigotry."[8]**

Adopted by the General Board, American Baptist Churches of the USA, on November 18, 2001.

he said that when "Americans become followers of Islam, [it] is nothing short of insanity . . . the Islamic people, the Arabs, were the ones who captured Africans, put them into slavery, and sent them to America as slaves. Why would people want to embrace the religion of the slavers?"[7] The Interfaith Alliance (TIA), a national grassroots organization dedicated to promoting the positive role of religion in public life, called on Robertson to recant his statements. "Robertson's remarks are offensive not only to the millions of American Muslims, but to people of faith throughout our country," says Rabbi Arthur Hertzberg, a national board member of TIA. "This type of religious bigotry is designed to pit Americans of various faith traditions against one another, rather than bring us all together."

"What Mr. Robertson seems to be telling us, is that in order to be a true American, one must not only be a Christian, but his type of Christian," says TIA spokesperson Mohamad Elleithee. "Fortunately, most Americans reject this type of religious intolerance and recognize the positive contributions that all people of Faith have made to our country."[9]

Of course, Islam is not the only religion that has been attacked. As the ADL reports in its 2001 survey, anti-Semitism is on the rise. Christianity itself has often been assailed by groups ranging from atheists to pagans (those who practice witchcraft). In the past and present, Catholics have been stereotyped and discriminated against by Protestants and members of other religious groups. Followers of the Church of Jesus Christ of Latter Day Saints (Mormons) are no strangers to bigotry, having lived with persecution during the nineteenth and part of the twentieth centuries. Scientology, a recent religion whose philosophy was formed by author L. Ron Hubbard, has frequently been stereotyped as a cult and the church has been harassed by citizen groups as well as by local governments.

There probably is not an organized religion of any kind in the United States that has not been the target of some type of bigotry and prejudicial actions. But religious conflicts are not limited to questions about whose way of life is "right" and whose god will lead the way to paradise. Some of the most recent religious debates have centered on public schools.

RELIGIOUS DIVERSITY IN PUBLIC SCHOOLS

Should creationism—the belief that the world and humankind were created literally as described in the biblical book of Genesis—be taught in public schools? Should tax funds be used for transporting students to parochial schools—those operated by religious groups? Should tax money be used to support voucher programs, providing funds so students can attend private schools rather than public schools in an effort to improve their education? Should students be allowed to organize religious clubs and use public schools for their meetings? Should prayer be allowed in public school ceremonies?

The latter question has probably raised more furor across the United States than any other related to religious liberty and public schools. One of the most significant decisions was the U.S. Supreme Court ruling in *Engel v. Vitale* (1962). The case came about because the New York State Board of Regents, the governing body for New York's schools, had established a program for moral and spiritual training. The regents composed a nondenominational prayer that students were supposed to recite each morning. But parents of ten students in the New York public schools charged that the practice was unconstitutional. Eight out of nine of the U.S. justices agreed.

THE MAJORITY DECISION

Justice Hugo Black wrote the majority decision in *Engel v. Vitale*. He took great care to point out that the authors of the U.S. Constitution and the Bill of Rights knew that the First Amendment, which tried to put an end to governmental control of religion and of prayer, was not written

> **to destroy either. They knew rather that it was written to quiet well justified fears which nearly all of them felt arising out of an awareness that governments of the past had shackled men's tongues to make them speak only the religious thoughts that government wanted them to speak and to pray only to the god that government wanted them to pray to. It is neither sacrilegious nor antireligious to say that each separate government in this country should stay out of the business of writing or sanctioning official prayers and leave that purely religious function to the people themselves and to those the people choose to look to for religious guidance.[10]**

Many Americans adamantly protested; some even predicted that the nation was headed for ruin if not doomed to hell. The plaintiffs in the case were viciously attacked with hate calls and death threats.

Some members of Congress tried to reverse the Court decision by drafting constitutional amendments to reinstate prayer in the public schools. However, there was not enough support to change the U.S. Constitution.

AN ONGOING ISSUE

School prayer issues did not disappear over the next forty years. Among the contested issues have been prayers at public school graduation ceremonies. Traditionally, the prayers were offered by Christian ministers or priests. But graduating public school students include Unitarians, Jews, Muslims, Hindus, and members of other religious groups, as well as atheists. Should a graduation ceremony begin with a prayer that some students would find offensive or cause them discomfort?

To deal with the question, some schools ask clerics to recite nondenominational prayers. But legal experts argue that prayer—no matter how neutral it might be—in a public school is, because of the setting, tantamount to a government-sponsored prayer and thus unconstitutional. On the other side, supporters contend that graduation prayers should be allowed because they are traditional and inspire graduates.

Cases have been argued in various state and federal appellate courts. In one instance, Robert E. Lee, a public school principal, invited a rabbi to offer prayer at a graduation ceremony. Lee gave the rabbi a pamphlet containing guidelines for the composition of public prayers at civic ceremonies and advised him that the prayers should be nonsectarian. Daniel Weisman, whose daughter was a student at the school, sought a temporary restraining order to prohibit school officials from including the prayers in the ceremony. Although the petition was denied, Weisman later won a permanent injunction in the District Court, which ruled that the practice at issue violated the establishment clause.

Public school officials appealed to the U.S. Supreme Court, and the justices ruled on the case *Lee v. Weisman* in 1992. In a 5 to 4 decision, the Court stated, in part:

> *The school district's supervision and control of a high school graduation ceremony places subtle and indirect public and peer pressure on attending students to stand as a group or maintain respectful silence during the invocation and benediction. A reasonable dissenter of high school age could believe that standing or remaining silent signified her own participation in, or approval of, the group exercise, rather than her respect for it. And the State may not place the student dissenter in the dilemma of participating or protesting. Since adolescents are often susceptible to peer pressure, especially in matters of social convention, the State may no more use social pressure to enforce orthodoxy than it may use direct means.*[11]

Although this ruling extended the ban against prayer in public school settings, still other cases have broken through the "wall of separation." An example is the Supreme Court's 2001 ruling in *Good News Club v. Milford Central School* (in New York state) that allows evangelical Bible clubs to use public school facilities to hold their meetings.[12]

POLITICS AND RELIGIOUS DIVERSITY

Religious activities in public schools make up just one facet of the many political issues affected by Americans's religious beliefs. Today, in the public arena it is commonplace to focus on the religious components of such issues as abortion, cloning, sex education, gay and lesbian rights, assisting terminally ill patients to die, religious symbols on public property, book banning, pornography, illicit drugs, and waging war.

One of the most recent public concerns is over a court decision to ban as unconstitutional the words "under God" from the pledge of allegiance to the U.S. flag. In July 2002, the ninth U.S. Circuit Court of Appeals ruled that the phrase "under God," which was added to the pledge in 1954, is unconstitutional because it endorses religion. While this decision prompted a huge outcry from the American public and politicians, some groups praised the decision, among them Americans United for Separation of Church and State. In the opinion of Barry W. Lynn, the executive director of the organization, the "decision shows respect for freedom of conscience. You can be a patriotic

"A UNIQUE FORCE IN SOCIETY"

Religious diversity plays a role in numerous political concerns, and a posting on Tolerance.org sums up the fact that "[r]eligion is a unique force in society":

It promotes both good and evil. Historically, it has helped to abolish slavery. It has promoted racial integration, equal rights for women, and equal rights for gays and lesbians. It has motivated individuals to create massive support services for the poor, the sick, the hurting, and the broken. Conversely, it has been used to justify slavery, racial segregation, oppression of women, discrimination against homosexuals, genocide, extermination of minorities, and other horrendous evils.

Religion drives some to dedicate their lives to help the poor and needy. . . . It drives others to exterminate as many "heretics" as they can. . . . Religion has the capability to generate unselfish love in some people, and vicious, raw hatred in others.

American regardless of your religious belief or lack of religion," he says. "Our government should never coerce [anyone] to make a profession of religious belief. America is an incredibly diverse country with some 2,000 different religions and denominations, as well as millions of Americans who profess no religion at all. Government actions should respect that diversity."[13]

Many people believe that the increasing diversity in the United States—whether religious or otherwise—is a force for social good. But at the same time, the nation's cultural diversity has spawned "raw hatred" and prompted vicious crimes. As mass crimes and genocide caused by differences in religious beliefs have taken place in other parts of the world, such as Afghanistan, Bosnia, Kosovo, Northern Ireland, Pakistan, the Philippines, and other countries, some Americans wonder how those who do not abide by the doctrines of religious zealots will fare in a culturally and religiously diverse nation.

WHAT DO YOU THINK?

"I really believe that the pagans and the abortionists and the feminists and the gays and the lesbians who are actively trying to make that an alternative lifestyle, the ACLU, People for the American Way, all of them who try to secularize America. . . . I point the finger in their face and say you helped this happen." These are the words of evangelist Jerry Falwell who appeared on Pat Robertson's 700 Club show just two days after the terrorist attacks on September 11, 2001. Robertson said, "I totally concur."

The president for the People for the American Way immediately expressed his concern, "At a time when political leaders of both parties are urging bipartisanship and national unity, it is truly unfortunate that Americans who watched [the September 13] edition of Pat Robertson's 700 Club television program received a far different message. . . . This is a time for a shared national commitment to bringing those responsible for the terrorist attacks to justice. It is also a time to renew our commitment to protecting the constitutional liberties and democratic values that sustain our free society."[14]

Whose message was on the mark? What do you think?

During the 1920s, Clarence Darrow defended John T. Scopes, a biology teacher in Tennessee, who taught the theory of evolution, which was prohibited by state law at the time. Photo courtesy of the Library of Congress.

RELIGIOUS FREEDOM

To underscore the importance of religious freedom guaranteed by the U.S. Constitution, imagine what life might be like without it. Suppose the nation was governed by a religious group called the Do-Gooders. To be respected by the majority in this imaginary society, you would have to be a Do-Gooder. Like all Do-Gooders, you would be required to post a list of Do-Good rules in your home and read the rules aloud twice each day. The rules would require that Do-Gooders wear smile buttons to show they were part of the religious order. Those not part of the order would be required to wear cone-shaped hats, marking them as Dunces.

No public dissent would be allowed in Do-Good land. All families would be required to support religious schools, and all young people would have to attend them, even the Dunces. If you were a Do-Gooder, however, you would not be allowed to associate with the Dunces, but you would be allowed to publicize their misdeeds.

Obviously, if Do-Gooders were in charge many other rules could be added. The point is, if a religious majority gains enough power, it can force its beliefs on others. The U.S. Constitution guards against that and protects religious freedom.

6 From Intolerance, to Hatred, to Violence

It is disheartening and damaging to the human sprit to know that we are dragging . . . racism, intolerance and hatred into a new century.

—Terrell Jones, vice provost for educational equity at Pennsylvania State University[1]

Thousands of incidents of intolerance and hatred—and increasing violence—have occurred since 2000. Just a few news stories from cities across the United States reflect the trend:

- A rash of hate mail was sent to African American athletes, students, and a member of Pennsylvania State University's Board of Directors at the beginning of 2000.
- In Ithaca, New York, in July 2002, "Three local white residents [were] charged with viciously assaulting an African American woman in a racially motivated attack. . . . The victim told police she was walking home from work when she heard people yelling, 'Nigger' and other racial slurs at her from the back of a Ford pickup truck, according to police reports."[2]
- In 2002, "A federal grand jury . . . indicted a Maryland man on charges of murdering two female hikers in Virginia in 1996 after the man said they 'deserved to die' for being lesbians. . . . Darrell David Rice, 34, of Columbia, Md. . . . has committed numerous physical and verbal assaults against randomly selected women, and said he chose women 'because they are more vulnerable than men.' He also said he 'hates gays.'"[3]
- The National Asian Pacific American Legal Consortium (NAPALC) "documented nearly 250 bias-motivated incidents targeting Asian Pacific Americans (APAs) generally and South Asians particularly in the three-month period following September 11 [2001]. . . . At least two APAs were murdered as part of the backlash. . . . An alarming number of the post 9–11 backlash incidents against APAs occurred in schools

and in the workplace. In a number of cases, students were the targets of racial slurs by their classmates, and some were even physically attacked while at school. Workplace incidents involved threatening phone calls, racial epithets inflicted by co-workers, and actual physical assaults suffered by APA victims."[4]

- In Lancaster, California, on February 12, 2002, "Alan Elmus Hall and Antoine Bohannon, both 18, and a 17-year-old boy were charged with battery causing serious bodily harm after allegedly yelling racial epithets while attacking a biracial boy."[5]
- In April 2002, Hector Arturo Diaz of Sunland Park, New Mexico, was shot in the back. A cross-dresser, Diaz was dressed in female clothing and his body was left in a parking lot. Police arrested and charged twenty-year-old Justen Grant Hall of Texas with the hate crime.
- Members of the Church of the Knights of the Ku Klux Klan (KKK) held a "White Pride Festival" on a farm in northern Indiana during the first weekend in August 2002. The event, which was similar to other hate-group gatherings, included the bands Fueled by Hate, Definite Hate, SS 187, and Defenders of the Faith. Along with the farm owner Richard Loy, the KKK grand dragon of Indiana, guest speakers included white supremacist Tom Metzger, who leads the White Aryan Resistance (WAR); Matt Hale, the leader of the Church of the Creator, which is not a church but a white supremacist organization; Ray Larsen, the imperial wizard of the National Knights of the KKK; Ron Edwards, the imperial wizard of the Imperial Klans of America; and neo-Nazi Ted Dunn from the SS Action Group.[6]

What can be done about the hate groups that sponsor "festivals" and spread their white supremacist attitudes and venomous hatred around the world? "Censorship is not the answer," according to the Anti-Defamation League (ADL). "ADL supports the free speech guarantees embodied in the

First Amendment of the United States Constitution, believing that the best way to combat hateful speech is with more speech."[7]

The ADL along with groups such as the Intelligence Center of the Southern Poverty Law Center (SPLC), the Center for New Community, the Prejudice Institute, the NAPALC, the Simon Wiesenthal Center, the National Association for the Advancement of Colored People (NAACP), the Center for Democratic Renewal, and other civil rights organizations monitor hate on the Internet and the hatemongers themselves to expose their propaganda and lies. Most antihate organizations have websites and publish materials that present factual information about those who are attempting to destroy nonwhite and non-Christian citizens of the United States—and in some cases the U.S. government itself.

WHAT'S IN A NAME?

Hate groups in the United States operate under many different names, some of them purporting to be religious or patriotic in nature and seemingly harmless. Here are some examples with brief descriptions of their activities:

American Patrol/Voice of Citizens Together—This anti-immigration group has a bigoted and anti-Latino agenda.

Black African Holocaust Council—Led by a Nation of Islam member, the group often blames Jews and Jewish organizations for a variety of plots supposedly designed to destroy the black community.

Council of Conservative Citizens—This is a racist political group.

Institute for Historical Review—Known for its neo-Nazi views, the leaders of this group deny that during World War II the Nazis murdered millions of Jews in what is now known as the Holocaust. They argue that the Holocaust was a hoax in spite of abundant evidence to the contrary.

National Organization for European American Rights—A racist and anti-Semitic group, it was founded by former Klansman David Duke, who has consistently spouted his hate rhetoric for three decades.

Society to Remove All Immoral Godless Homosexual Trash—As its title suggests, this group focuses hatred on gays and lesbians.

Patriots—Numerous groups, many of them racist, call themselves part of the Patriot movement, which is based on hate for the federal government and a belief that government officials are conspiring against them. Most Patriots are members of militias and train for armed resistance.

The Nuremberg Files—This antiabortion website lists abortion providers and appears to target them for elimination, crossing out the names of abortionists and their supporters who have been killed.

Church of the Creator—White supremacists who consider themselves a religious group founded on the proposition that the white race is "nature's highest creation" and that "white people are the creators of all worthwhile culture and civilization."

For years, members of the Ku Klux Klan, one of the oldest hate groups, have marched to call attention to their white supremacist views. Photo courtesy of the Southern Poverty Law Center.

SOME HATEMONGERS

The SPLC's Intelligence Project documented 708 active hate groups in 2002, most of them in California, Texas, Florida, and other southern states. Groups are also scattered across the United States, as a map posted in its *Intelligence Report* magazine and on its Internet site shows.

The KKK is one of the oldest and best known of the hate groups. It began after the Civil War and was led by a former Confederate general who preached white supremacy. Although the Klan was originally a social club of Confederate veterans who met in secret and disguised themselves in white robes and masks, it soon organized to spread a reign of terror across the south. KKK members attacked, maimed, and frequently killed newly enfranchised black Americans and anyone involved with government officials who had dismantled racist power structures.

Over the decades, KKK activities declined, revived, died out, and revived again. Always, Klan members proclaimed their view of white supremacy—meaning white Anglo-Saxon Protestant supremacy—by attacking not only African Americans, but also Jews, Catholics, and immigrants. Klan membership has dropped to a historic low in recent years, but other hate groups have evolved, sometimes recruiting from the Klan.

Many recruits join neo-Nazi groups, which include a variety of organizations and individuals worldwide who are inspired by the hate dogma of Adolf Hitler, the Nazi dictator who overran Europe during World War II. Though long dead, Hitler is considered a hero to neo-Nazis who celebrate the German dictator's birthday and preach his fascist, Nazi doctrine.

One of the most virulent of the neo-Nazi groups is the Aryan Nations, which once had a compound in Hayden Lake, Idaho. In recent times, the compound was sold to pay off millions of dollars that a court awarded to creditors in a lawsuit. Today, Aryan Nations has broken up into separate factions, and some observers worry that a new more powerful group will form to carry on violent white supremacist activities.

Aryan Nations began as the military arm of the Church of Jesus Christ Christian in the United States. The so-called church is part of the Christian Identity (or simply

IDENTITY BELIEFS

According to the Identity dogma, the biblical Adam fathered Abel, while Eve, Identity preachers say, had intercourse with a snake and produced Cain. According to this implausible story, Adam produced more children and Yahweh (a name for God) chose one of them, Abraham, to found the non-Jewish Nation of Israel. Abraham's grandson, Jacob, fathered twelve sons, who became the leaders of the twelve tribes of Israel. Ten of the tribes were captured by Assyrians and disappeared from biblical accounts, but the philosophy contends that these tribes became European settlers. One tribe eventually crossed the Atlantic Ocean, and God entrusted them with the Declaration of Independence, the U.S. Constitution, and the Bill of Rights.

Cain's descendants, Identity members claim, are the offspring of animals with whom Cain mated before he killed Abel. Cain created nonwhites known as "mud people." The so-called "true chosen people"—white Anglo-Saxons—must battle and destroy the mud people and the "children of Satan" who, Identity claims, are part of the Zionist Occupational Government (ZOG) that supposedly controls the United States.[8]

Identity) movement. Identity doctrine is based on bogus Christian teachings, maintaining that Anglo-Saxons, not Jews, are the biblical "chosen people."

Most militant white supremacist groups believe the illogical, bogus doctrine of Christian Identity, and among them are skinheads. However, not all skinheads are racists or fascists. Some skinheads simply dress and act like the 1960s' punk rock crowd or like street toughs. But over the past decade, skinheads connected with hate groups have been responsible for dozens of murders and hundreds of brutal attacks against nonwhites, non-Christians, homosexuals, and nonracist skinheads. Such an incident took place in Portland, Oregon, in late 2001 when racist skinhead James Torkelson and his buddies fought with nonracist skinheads. After the fight, police reported that Torkelson and others kidnapped a teenage girl, held her for several days, and beat her so severely that she was unrecognizable. Torkelson, who has ties with the Aryan Nations, fled the area and was harbored by a Klan group in Indiana. Police arrested Torkelson on New Year's Day 2002.[9]

WHITE ARYAN RESISTANCE

One of the most vicious hate groups is the White Aryan Resistance (WAR) masterminded by former Klan leader Tom Metzger and his son John, both of Fallbrook, California. In 1990, the Metzgers were convicted in a civil case of inciting skinheads to attack three Ethiopians in Portland, Oregon. The skinheads beat the Ethiopians with baseball bats, killing Mulugerta Seraw, a community college student in Portland. Three skinheads were convicted of the attack and one received a life sentence for the murder.

Although the Metzgers were not charged with the beatings and murder, the SPLC sued them on behalf of Seraw's family. A jury found them liable for the skinheads' actions and awarded the family $12 million. As a result, the Metzgers declared bankruptcy and WAR has lost some support. However, its website is still maintained, advertising "North America's most Racist Radical Newspaper W.A.R.";

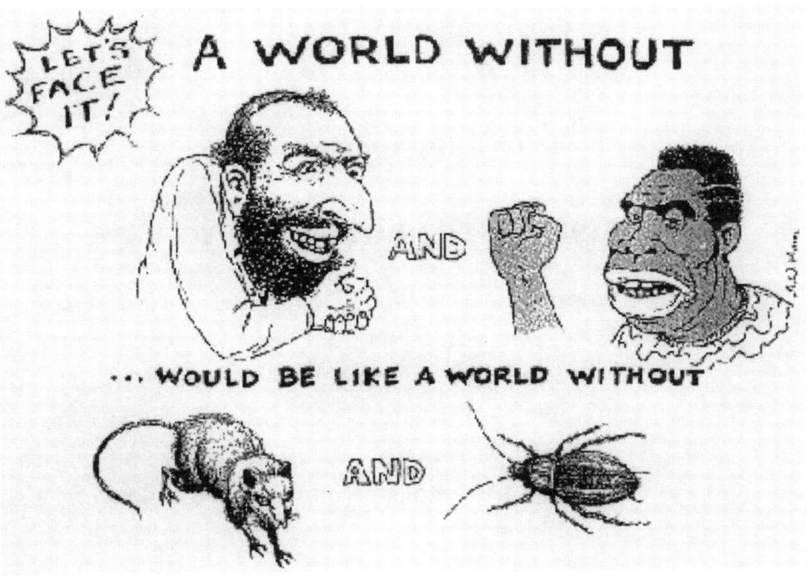

works by George Lincoln Rockwell, the founder of the American Nazi Party; and videos about Hitler. The website links to anti-Semitic diatribes and crude, disgusting cartoons whose labels clearly indicate their ugliness, "Spics, Greasers, Beaners, Wetbacks," "Moon Crickets, Niggers, Spades, Jigaboos," and "Kikes, Sheenies, Hebs, Roaches."

In order to inform the public about WAR's malicious attacks, the ADL includes on its website an example of a hateful cartoon. Although extremely offensive, the ADL notes that this example "most expressively represent Metzger's" and WAR's views.[10]

Among the hundreds of other hate groups is the National Alliance, a loosely organized network cofounded by the late William Pierce, who died in July 2002. Pierce, under the pseudonym Andrew Macdonald, published *The Turner Diaries* in 1978. Considered a bible for many neo-Nazis and other hate groups, the novel describes a guerrilla war against the U.S. government, people of color, and Jews. As the war intensifies, major U.S. cities are destroyed and the hero of the book flies a suicide mission into the Pentagon. In addition, it contains a description of a terrorist bombing that closely resembles the bombing of the Alfred P. Murrah Federal Building in Oklahoma City, Oklahoma, in 1995. Timothy McVeigh, who read the book and steeped himself in racist and antigovernment propaganda, was convicted and executed for the crime, which killed 168 people.

TURNING TEENAGERS ON TO HATE

According to the U.S. Department of Education, "Teenagers and young adults account for a significant proportion of the country's hate crimes both as perpetrators and as victims. Hate-motivated behavior, whether in the form of ethnic conflict, harassment, intimidation, or graffiti, is often apparent on school grounds. Hate violence is also perpetrated by hate groups, which actively work to recruit young people to their ranks."[11]

Floyd Cochran, a former racist and neo-Nazi, was turned on to hate when he was thirteen years old. Cochran grew up in foster homes in upstate New York and was attracted to the KKK because members treated him like family. According to a news report, Cochran "heard the dairy farmers he worked with rail against the government," just like the Klan did. "When they said God was a white supremacist, it wasn't much of a leap because in every picture I'd ever seen of God, he was white," he told a reporter.

However, Cochran said he didn't like wearing white sheets, so he left the KKK and joined the Aryan Nations at its compound in Couer D'Alene, Idaho. He became a spokesman for the neo-Nazis, spreading the group's beliefs and frequently recruiting outside schools. "I felt like I was an evangelist on a mission from God," he said.[12]

He eventually married and had a family. But in 1992, he left the Aryan Nations. Why? Because at a Nazi youth rally one member told Cochran that when the Aryan Nations and groups like them gained power, his son, who was born with a cleft palate and cleft lip, would be euthanized because he was marked as "inferior."

Today, Cochran travels the nation to educate and warn communities about the dangers of hate groups and their youth-recruitment tactics. He tells audiences, "We're all vulnerable in that if these young people grow into white supremacists, we could all be targets for attack."[13]

How do hate groups recruit? Not only with rallies and handouts, but also with music, video games, and websites. More than one hundred white power bands in North America "either express white supremacist ideas in their music or are involved with white supremacist organizations. Several musical genres are represented: "white power rock (Skinhead, Oi!, hatecore, metal, thrash, and rock varieties); National Socialist Black Metal; fascist experimental (goth, industrial, techno, 'apocalyptic' folk, and 'noise' varieties); and racist country and folk music," according to a report by the Center for New Community and the SPLC's *Intelligence Report.* White power rock bands go by such names as Aggravated Assault, Aggressive Force, Angry Aryans, Angry White Youth, Hatemonger, Kick to Kill, and White Terror. Other bands give themselves titles that range from Aryan Tormentor to Warcom.[14]

Check it out!

According to Devin Burghart, "[hate] music has become the most significant recruiting tool for the white supremacist movement."[15]

The largest distributor of hate music recordings is Resistance Records of Detroit, Michigan, which was started in 1993 by Canadian George Burdi, once a member of the neo-Nazi Church of the Creator (COTC). He also "edited *Resistance* magazine, sang for the band Rahowa (short for 'racial holy war,' the slogan of COTC), and became one of the world's most visible racists." According to Tolerance.org, "Burdi was imprisoned in 1997 in connection with the beating of a female anti-racist activist following a fiery Burdi speech in Ottawa. . . . After his release from prison, he cut all ties with the white power movement."

In 2001, an interviewer with *Intelligence Report* talked to Burdi, who told about his introduction to white supremacy when he was a university freshman and received a copy of *The White Man's Bible* written by Ben Klassen, the cofounder of the COTC. Burdi said, "I couldn't believe that that type of stuff even existed. I was turned off by it. . . . But I couldn't stop thinking about it. It said Jews and every other race look after their own interests first and foremost, and that it should be your responsibility as a young white person to promote your race first and foremost. Klassen was arguing that white people are the creators of civilization; that's why it's called the Church of the Creator."[16]

In the latter part of the interview with the *Intelligence Report* journalist, Burdi discussed the changes in his life after he got out of jail in 1997:

Intelligence Report: In what sense do you now feel racism is wrong?

Burdi: Racism is wrong . . . hatred is wrong, anger is wrong. Hatred and anger are wrong because they consume what is good in you. They smother your ability to appreciate love and peace. . . . [R]acism is wrong [because] you attach yourself to the accomplishments of white Europeans, instead of developing yourself and actually contributing to the society you live in.

Intelligence Report: You sang a song called "Third Reich" that includes these lyrics: "You kill all the niggers and you gas all the Jews; kill a gypsy and a commie, too. You just killed a kike, don't it feel right; goodness gracious, Third Reich." How does that song make you feel today?

Burdi: I didn't write the music or the lyrics for that song, I should say. The lyrics are incredibly negative, incredibly destructive to everyone mentioned in the song. They do a total disservice to anybody who thinks that the white power movement has any ideals beyond guttural hate. Frankly, I am quite ashamed that I ever participated in singing those lyrics. It would be impossible for me to make a personal apology to everyone who was ever affected by that song. But the people who bought it, they wanted to listen to it and probably already had those ideas in their heads.[17]

Although hate music is illegal in Canada and many European countries, it is protected in the United States as free speech by the Constitution's First Amendment. The music may be played by bands at white supremacist rallies or spread via the Internet.

A variety of hate groups use not only the Internet, but also other media such as cable television, short-wave radio, and published materials, including comic books and video games aimed at teenagers, to distribute their hate messages. To spread that message, the National Alliance produced a video game called *Ethnic Cleansing*, geared for males aged fifteen to thirty. Released in 2002 on Martin Luther King Day, the game shows a white-hooded Klansman as a hero killing African Americans in shirts with the words "Big Nig"; their deaths are accompanied by the sounds of screeching monkeys. An advertisement on National Alliance's website reads, "Run through the ghetto blasting away various blacks and spics in an attempt to gain entrance to the subway system . . . where the jews [*sic*] have hidden to avoid the carnage. Then if your [*sic*] lucky you can blow away jews as they scream 'Oy Vey!' on your way to their command center."[18]

WHAT DO YOU THINK?

A search on the Internet using the term "hate groups" brings up numerous websites that contain white supremacist harangues and virulent anti-Semitic diatribes. Debates have been ongoing for several years regarding the effect these sites have on viewers, particularly teenagers. On one side are those who think the sites should be closed down so decent people won't be corrupted by the propaganda. On the other side are those who believe that it's important to expose bigots and racists in order to inform the public about their irrational views that often lead to hate crimes.

Which side is on target? What do you think?

According to the ADL, such computer games are increasing. They are advertised as "entertainment" on extremist sites run by neo-Nazis, white supremacists, and Holocaust deniers. "Once again, racists are finding new ways to exploit technology to spread their message of white supremacy, anti-Semitism and hate to a mass audience," says Abraham H. Foxman, the ADL national director. "As with most computer games, these games are being created primarily for a teenage audience. The difference is these games are loaded with blatantly racist messages and themes. It's a disgusting, sick perversion of the original games, where the manipulated versions give players points for killing as many non-whites and Jews as possible."[19]

HATE CRIMES

Various federal and state laws define the term "hate crime," which generally refers to an attack on an individual or his or her property (for example, vandalism, arson, assault, or murder). The victim is intentionally selected because of his or her skin color, religion, national origin, gender, disability, or sexual orientation.

For example, in Elkhart, Indiana, Sasezley Richardson, a nineteen-year-old black youth, was shot to death while walking home from a mall. Richardson was killed in November 1999 in what police have called a hate crime linked to the Aryan Brotherhood, a white supremacist prison gang. Alex Witmer, who had spent time in juvenile prison, and Jason Powell were convicted of the crime. According to court testimony in January 2002, reported in the local press, "Powell had been 'talking about wanting to kill a black person to get what he thought was a symbol.' Witmer said he told Powell to either do it or quit talking about it. They got into Witmer's car and Witmer drove. Witmer's .22 caliber rifle was in the car and Witmer said Powell picked it up and held it in his lap."

Witmer drove along a mall where he and Powell saw Richardson walking and followed him into the neighborhood where he lived. When they spotted Richardson again, Powell fired the rifle—a dozen times. Witmer did nothing to stop his friend. And Richardson died because two people hated the color of his skin.[20]

7 Reducing Bigotry, Racism, and Hate Crimes

The Asian girls in my class have hung out with me and asked questions about my culture. . . . The relationship between blacks and Chinese has really changed a lot.

—Jo-Anne Henderson, a black teenager in Chicago[1]

With websites, musical lyrics, cartoons, and published materials spewing hate, it's easy to assume that very few people are attempting to reduce bigotry, prejudice, and racism. But take another look. Individuals and groups, many of them involving teenagers, are doing their part to stop the hate and improve the way people of diverse backgrounds relate to one another.

Websites are an important factor in spreading the word about efforts to stop hate. Search terms such as "stop hate," "fighting hate," and "antiracism" will bring up hundreds of pages and sites that provide examples of what people can do to counteract hatemongers.

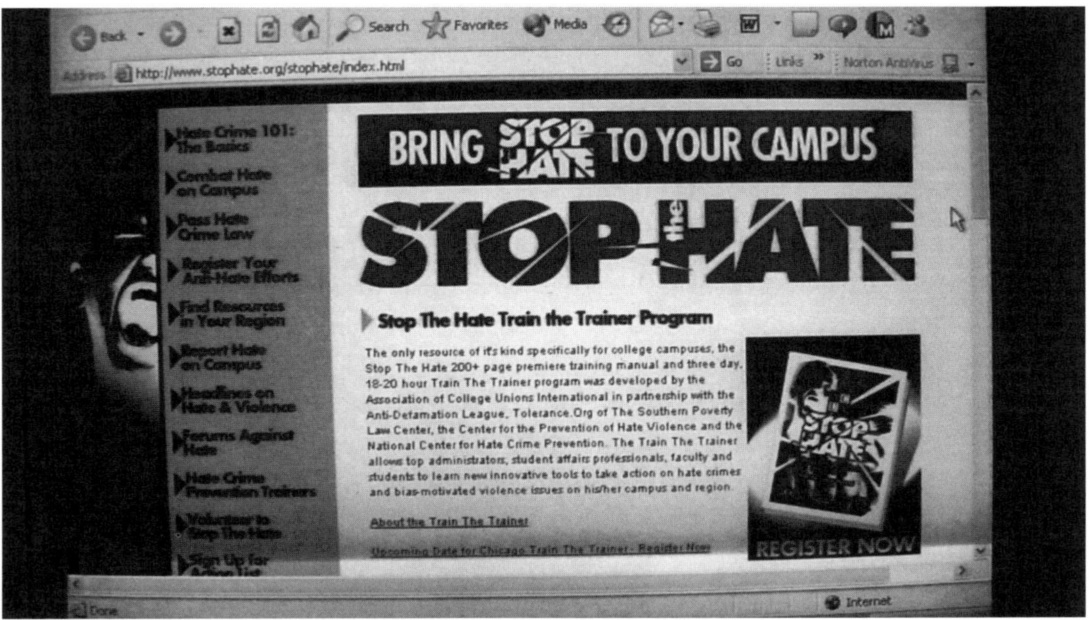

Stop the Hate is a website with lots of information on how to combat hate on school campuses. Photo by the author.

ANYTOWN USA

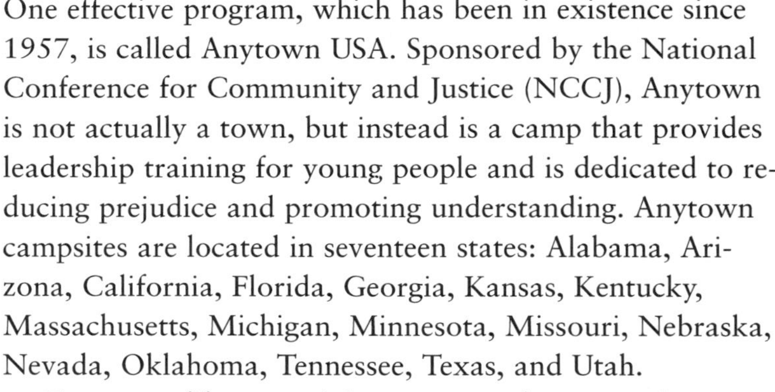

One effective program, which has been in existence since 1957, is called Anytown USA. Sponsored by the National Conference for Community and Justice (NCCJ), Anytown is not actually a town, but instead is a camp that provides leadership training for young people and is dedicated to reducing prejudice and promoting understanding. Anytown campsites are located in seventeen states: Alabama, Arizona, California, Florida, Georgia, Kansas, Kentucky, Massachusetts, Michigan, Minnesota, Missouri, Nebraska, Nevada, Oklahoma, Tennessee, Texas, and Utah.

Teenagers fifteen to eighteen years of age complete an application to become a delegate—that is, a representative of her or his school and community. Students must obtain a letter of recommendation from an adult at their school, house of worship, or organization at which they have volunteered. Depending on the location of the camp, costs can range from $200 to $500, but accepted delegates often get financial help, if needed, from such sources as civic groups, religious organizations, and NCCJ scholarships.

At Anytown camps, teenagers of diverse religious, cultural, and ethnic backgrounds come together and learn to better understand themselves and others. In 2001, at least seventeen ethnicities and nineteen religious affiliations were represented in Anytown, Georgia, according to its website. The site opens with quotes from former delegates, such as "Because of Anytown I have a new sense of confidence that I can make a difference in my community," "I got a whole new family, an Anytown family," and "The people who taught me the most were the ones I wouldn't normally associate with at school. Now I know better."[2]

One alumni of Anytown in Massachusetts, Kate Crockford of Holliston High School in Boston, is featured on the website Stopthehate.org. The site is sponsored by the Governor's Task Force on Hate Crimes in Massachusetts and includes suggestions for actions students can take to reduce hate crimes. Kate has been involved in numerous activities to promote diversity and awareness of cultural differences

ANYTOWN

This excerpt from an article in the August 2001 *Community Update*, a monthly magazine published by the U.S. Department of Education, describes a Florida Anytown program:

> ***ANYTOWN—Community Program Changes Tampa Youth from the Inside Out***
> ***By Nicole Ashby***
>
> ***Vicki and Louie Cazares immediately recognized the difference in their teenage daughter after she returned from "Anytown," a leadership retreat near their Tampa, Fla., home. "When your child comes home and tells you she had a 'life-changing experience,' you can't help but take notice," says her mother. Once shy, Renae had risen in confidence, joining a local youth committee, embracing persons whom before she had not. The change was so striking that next summer the Cazareses sent their son for the experience.***
>
> ***Like Renae, many youths, along with their families and schools, testify to the transforming power of Anytown. A week-long program, Anytown brings together a mix of high school students to help them identify who they are, what they believe, and how to act on those beliefs. . . . "If we just let people live in their own little isolated hamlets, they're never going to break down . . . stereotypes," explains Roy Kaplan, executive director of NCCJ's Tampa Bay region. . . .***
>
> ***Witnessing a difference among Anytown graduates, school systems want to send more students to the program. . . . "We've all become much more aware of the need to give our students some tools that go beyond reading and math," says Candy Olson, a member of the Hillsborough County School Board, whose daughter also went through Anytown. . . .***
>
> ***In a week packed with exercises and discussion groups that take up issues from racism to ageism, Anytowners come to understand their own biases as they learn to break down the stereotypes that cause discord. . . . The students' values are constantly tested in activities and dialogues, including talks about the Middle Passage, Holocaust, and Japanese internment, which provide a larger lens of prejudices that exist outside their own.***
>
> ***"Anytown isn't about telling kids what to think," says Margarita Sarmiento, associate director of NCCJ Tampa Bay. "It encourages kids to determine what they believe. And once they determine what they believe, [they] determine how they're going to stand up for what they believe in." She says the goal is to mold leaders, instead of crowd pleasers, who will care about social justice.***
>
> ***"These kids are gonna change the world," Kaplan says, though he admits the change is not always immediately received in their hometowns. "Are we going to completely reverse racism? No, but we're going to show that there are good people in every community and that we can work together for the common good."[3]***

and the need for tolerance. When she was a junior in high school, she started a group called Gay Straight Alliance (GSA). According to a profile of Kate posted on the website:

> *The first year was tough and took a lot of dedication, commitment, and effort to get the club going. For most of the year, Kate was the only consistent member and four to five students would attend meetings from time to*

time. In an attempt to reach more of the masses, she decided the GSA would fight against all forms of prejudice . . . [and] collaborated with Amnesty International in organizing Harmony Week that tackled different "isms" each day. The most profound day of the week was the day of silence that showed students how some silently suffer and seem invisible while daily insults and threats abound. Fifty students and two teachers wore black for the day, and all were silent. The impact could be seen almost immediately as the final GSA meetings were filled with 30–50 students per meeting.[4]

DAY OF SILENCE

The "Day of Silence" was initiated in 1996 by eighteen-year-old University of Virginia student Maria Pulzetti. She wanted to create safer schools and to support the rights of lesbian, gay, bisexual, and transgendered people. More than 150 students took part in the first event, vowing to remain silent for the day and carrying cards explaining why they would not speak. Remaining silent demonstrated that many young people have no voice and must keep their sexual preferences secret—that is, stay in the closet—to avoid harassment, prejudice, discrimination, and even violence. The local press covered the event, which was so successful that during the following year, Pulzetti and Jessie Gilliam, then nineteen, developed a website and the idea spread across the United States and even to other countries.

In April each year, thousands of student volunteers in high schools and colleges now observe a National Day of Silence. Jared Phillips, a sixteen-year-old student at Kestrel High School in Prescott, Arizona, explains why he has participated, "I don't like hearing 'faggot' and 'dyke,' but that level of discrimination is acceptable [at schools today]. I'd hate to think that I would have doors closed because I'm gay. By not standing up and saying this is wrong, you can bet this is going to come around to you someday."[5]

According to *The Advocate,* a national gay and lesbian news magazine, students who participate in the Day of Silence get their messages "across loud and clear." In fact, teens who have organized the event in the past say that the broad participation of straight allies elevates the Day of Silence from "a bunch of gay kids complaining about discrimination to a formidable student-led movement for civil rights."[6]

The program has also helped students such as fifteen-year-old Nikira Hernandez of California. A member of the Rainbow Alliance, she organized her school's first Day of Silence in 2001. Before the event, the "Rainbow Alliance counted about half a dozen students as members—and they weren't very motivated. But when more than 200 people fell silent on their behalf . . . she couldn't believe how much her life changed." She told a reporter for *The Advocate,* "Seeing how many allies we had made me feel much more accepted at my school."[7]

NOT IN OUR TOWN

> Not in Our Town
> Not in Our State
> Idaho is Too Great for Hate

This message was printed on posters distributed throughout Idaho in 2001 by human rights organizations. The poster was a response to hate literature that was passed out in Boise, Idaho, neighborhoods, which previously had been subjected to such a campaign. "Frankly, these groups come here to distribute their hate literature because they believe that they have a sympathetic audience," says Susan Curtis, president of a county human rights task force. "We believe strongly that the vast majority of Idahoans really do want to stand up and say, 'No! Not in our state!'" The poster has been used "in an ongoing, visible manner" to counter hate incidents.[8]

Idaho's poster also reflects a "Not in Our Town" effort that took place in Billings, Montana, in 1992. At the time, hilltop rocks overlooking the city had been painted with racist and anti-Semitic graffiti. Police Chief Wayne Inman ordered city workers to clean up the rocks, but more graffiti and racist leaflets appeared and homes and businesses were vandalized. The community began to organize to help victims. Labor union members, for example, helped repaint a Native American home that had been damaged by graffiti. An African Methodist Episcopal Church was vandalized by skinheads, but members of predominantly white churches began to attend the African American church to lend support. When a cement block was thrown through the window of a Jewish home where a Menorah was being displayed, the local newspaper published a full-page picture of the candelabrum used in Jewish worship; thousands of Jews and non-Jews cut out the photograph and displayed the Menorah in their living room windows as a sign of unity. Other signs appeared, declaring, "Not in Our Town. No Hate." Citizens formed solidarity groups to combat attacks that were linked to skinheads, Aryan Nations, and Klan members and eventually put an end to the crimes.[9]

The Billings effort became the subject of a PBS documentary aired in 1995. In conjunction with the film *Not-in-Our-Town* (*NIOT*), campaigns were held in various cities across the United States. Two new versions of the documentary, *NIOT II* and *NIOT III,* were created. The latter, *Not-in-Our Town: The Story Continues,* premiered in September 2002, and the Our Town Campaign joined with Participate America Foundation's National Civic Participation Week, September 11–17, 2002, sharing the goal of educating Americans about the link between civic participation and American democracy.

The latest *NIOT* film includes the story about how students at a Jewish school in Los Altos, California, raised funds to help restore a predominantly Arab American church that had been torched by an arsonist. Included also is a profile of a "Not in Our School" campaign organized by twenty-five student council members of a middle school in Rockford, Illinois. Numerous other examples of NIOT activities from across the United States can be found on the Internet.[10]

READ ALL ABOUT IT!

At the beginning of the 2001 school year in Chicago, Illinois, Mayor Richard M. Daley announced a "One Book, One Chicago" program to encourage community-wide reading and discussion of his favorite book *To Kill a Mockingbird.* Published in 1960, this novel by Lee Harper is called a classic, a book for all ages. It won a Pulitzer Prize and has been published in hardcover and paperback and as an audio tape, CD, and e-book. It was the basis for a 1962 Academy Award–winning film starring Gregory Peck, which is available on videocassette. Today's high school social studies and English teachers assign the novel for student reviews and analysis. Numerous websites are devoted to excerpts, comments, and study notes regarding this book.

Why is this novel still being touted, read, heard on audio renditions, and seen on film? Because even though it is set in the 1930s in a small Alabama town, the damaging effects of racism, ignorance, and abuse, as dramatically portrayed in the book and film, ring true in many cases today. In fact, one reviewer in 2002 noted, "I've read the book three times in my life, at ages 13, 18, and 22. With each reading I gain a better appreciation for the storyline, the author, and the moral beliefs that are challenged within these pages. . . . [N]o matter how many times this novel is read, the reader will never cease to feel compelled by the message that it delivers."[11]

In the fictional account, a black man (Tom Robinson) is falsely accused of raping a white woman, and he's defended by a white lawyer (Atticus Finch), raising the ire of the racist southern community and inflicting harassment and discrimination against the lawyer's children, known as Scout and Jem in the book. But that's only one part of the story. Other aspects deal with such issues as treating people with idiosyncrasies (such as the reclusive neighbor Boo Radley) as humans and not losing faith in the good qualities of people in spite of prejudice and hatred.

MORE GROUPS AT WORK

Suggestions on how to reduce bigotry, prejudice, and hatred are available from many other nonprofit organizations—national, regional, state, and local. Also offering help are various government agencies, such as the U.S. Department of Justice and the U.S. Department of Education, the Massachusetts' Governor's Task Force on Hate Crimes, and various county and state human relations departments. In addition, an increasing number of online organizations are working toward stopping bigotry and hatred. One is the Civilrights.org, which maintains an online social justice network "committed to the continued pursuit of equality and fostering greater understanding and mutual respect for difference."

A well-known nonprofit organization fighting hate is the Southern Poverty Law Center (SPLC), which sponsors Tolerance.org, a website that "awakens people to the problems of hate and intolerance" and encourages them to take action. The SPLC publication *Ten Ways to Fight Hate* is a guide for communities, with sections on "Act" (do something in the face of hatred), "Unite" (organize allies)," "Support the Victims," "Do Your Homework," "Create an Alternative," "Speak Up," "Lobby Leaders," "Look Long Range," "Teach Tolerance," and "Dig Deeper." The Teaching Tolerance project of the SPLC publishes *Teaching Tolerance* magazine, which provides ideas for classroom projects promoting appreciation for diversity and the values of democracy. And its *Intelligence Report* describes hate group activities throughout the United States.

Other resources for materials that assist schools, civic groups, and communities to counter hate and discriminatory behavior include the Anti-Defamation League's (ADL) online catalog, which contains lists of books, guides, posters, and videos that aid in diversity appreciation. The ADL's *Prejudice: 101 Ways You Can Beat It! A Citizen's Action Guide* is also available on its site. On the Internet, Partners Against Hate has a Promising Programs Database, which presents innovative programs aimed at confronting bigotry and discrimination.

Young African-Americans Against Media Stereotypes (YAAAMS) is a fairly new organization that monitors "media coverage for fairness and accuracy" and documents African American stereotypes, which occur ten times more frequently than stereotypes of other groups. The YAAAMS website notes:

> *For years, the media has portrayed many African-Americans as criminals, gangbangers, welfare recipients, sex and drug addicts, and other unsavory characters. We believe this coverage is part of the reason why there is a negative image of African-Americans. More importantly*

. . . it is not so much what others think of us, but what many of us are thinking of ourselves. We have a whole generation of young African-Americans thinking that the only thing they can be is a professional athlete, actor, singer, rapper, comedian, or gangster. These roles constitute most of what we see of young African-Americans in the media. There have been improvements in the media over the years, but a lot of damage has already been done.[12]

EFFECTIVE STATE AND LOCAL GROUPS

There are effective state and local groups as well. For example, in St. Petersburg, Florida, a group of about fifty Northeast High School students—black, white, Hispanic, Asian, Serbian Orthodox, Jewish, Muslim, and Christian—met for more than a year to try to resolve differences and ease cultural strife. Roy Kaplan, the executive director of the Tampa area National Conference for Community and Justice, worked with the students, helping them to listen to and understand their peers. During their meetings, the students expressed frustration because "their teachers and peers don't always understand different cultures" and "talked about the need for a curriculum to address events such as the war in former Yugoslavia which greatly affected Bosnian and Serbian students." American-born students, on the other hand, felt no personal connection to faraway battles. But through the meetings, students began to talk to one another and plan projects, such as poster campaigns and roundtable discussions, to reduce discrimination and gain respect for diverse cultures. "My voice and her voice and his voice can make something different in the world," one student Nidal Hamed notes. "We need

MORE ORGANIZATIONS

The following is a sampling of other organizations offering ways to fight bigotry and racism:

- **American-Arab Anti-discrimination Committee**
- **CityKids Foundation**
- **Honor Our Neighbors Origins and Rights**
- **National Association for the Advancement of Colored People**
- **National Conference for Community and Justice**
- **National Gay and Lesbian Task Forces**
- **Rethinking Schools**
- **Simon Wiesenthal Center**

to teach other kids to love each other so we can have more peace in the world."[13]

In St. Louis, Missouri, the Diversity Awareness Partnership (DAP) is a public education effort that includes more than a dozen area businesses and community groups. DAP promotes the value of difference with a public awareness campaign. One aspect of the campaign features players with the St. Louis Rams, Blues, and Cardinals sending the message in commercials and on posters, "Make a difference by accepting everyone else's."

BRIDGES at the University of North Dakota (UND) is a student organization "committed to fighting racism and the systems which make it possible." BRIDGES's website points out:

> *One such system is the very school name of UND, the "Fighting Sioux." Whereas many students see the name being used in a respectful manner, BRIDGES understands that using any ethnic group as a moniker for a sports team is not respectful—it is exploitive and leads to dangerous stereotypes and, subsequently, racism . . . racism against Native peoples and the tradition of keeping them only as a mascot. There was also a tradition in feudalism, slavery, and the oppression of women. Once humanity recognized this was wrong, such practices began to change. Only after recognizing the harm of using human beings as mascots and placing them in precarious proximity to the ever-waiting "Sioux Suck!" call at a sporting event, will healing on all sides begin.*[14]

Another local group is the Cultural Diversity Network in Owatonna, Minnesota. The network conducts orientation sessions for Somali and Hispanic immigrants and links community volunteers with people interested in learning the English language. Another focus of the network is literacy, and "reading parties" are held in ethnic neighborhoods one evening per month during the summer. Through these parties, youth and adults of diverse cultural backgrounds get to know each other.

Addresses and websites for selected resource organizations and government agencies are listed in the appendix. However, as the U.S. Department of Justice cautions, "No one approach exists to confronting and preventing hate crimes in this nation. Rather, hate crimes will only be successfully addressed when countless people throughout the fifty states work together to develop approaches that are appropriate for their local communities and work individually to develop the courage and skills to serve as role models of civility and respect."[15]

8 Respecting Diversity

I am really getting tired of the racist jokes in my human behavior class.

—Tiki Wilson, VOX

In April 2002, news reports in print and on television (TV) reminded the general public that ten years earlier, in 1992, one of the nation's most destructive riots erupted in the south-central district of Los Angles, California. Fifty-five people were killed, more than 2,300 were injured, and damages totaled an estimated $1 billion. The riot was sparked by the acquittal of four white policemen involved in a horrific beating of black motorist Rodney King; police had pulled King over after a high-speed chase on a California freeway. George Holliday was standing on the balcony of a nearby building and videotaped the police surrounding King and clubbing him fifty-two times with their nightsticks, using a stun gun on him, and kicking him. As a result of the beating, King suffered eleven skull fractures and brain and kidney damage.

Holliday sent his tape to a local TV station, and soon the entire country viewed what the majority assumed was obvious police brutality. But in a trial a year later, an all-white jury in rural Simi, California, found the four defendants not guilty of assault and use of excessive force. That's when "all hell broke loose," as CNN reported. During the height of the riot, King appeared on TV to plead for people to be calm. "Can we all get along?" he asked plaintively. Over the years, his question has been repeated by many others, particularly those who work to gain respect for cultural differences and to diffuse cultural conflicts.

CAN WE ALL GET ALONG?

Teenagers have plenty of opinions about whether people of diverse cultural backgrounds can respect one another in spite of differences in skin color, beliefs, and customs. To white teenager Katie Roberts of Evansville, Wisconsin, it's a simple matter, "I think . . . that having different cultures is a good thing. If everyone were the same, life as we know it would be extremely boring," she writes.[1] Black teenager Cierra Benton in Chicago has little patience with people who don't get along. In her opinion, people "who are prejudice are in need of a lesson; they are worse than kids; they need to grow up and take a look at the world. There is more than one race, religion, etc. and they cannot change that so they need to get over it."[2]

College student Lisa Miller of Portland, Oregon, has a range of experiences about relating to people of diverse backgrounds—some positive, others negative. She recalls that she has known her best friend, who is Vietnamese, since third grade. Her friend stopped using her Vietnamese name "because the kids at school made fun of it." The two girls often were together, usually "hanging out" with white friends. But, Lisa writes, lately her friend "has been hanging out with a lot of Asians. . . . When we go out with her friends, they look at me funny, [as if to say] 'why are you hanging out with us—you aren't Asian.' Sometimes it can get a little weird."[3] Yet, as Lisa points out, people get together with those of their own culture "because those are the people that they have the most in common with. When I hang out with them I don't feel out of place so much because I am white, but more because I don't have any common experiences with them."

In Lisa's opinion, cultural conflicts come about because of misunderstandings. During her days at Portland's Grant High School where there was a mixture of white, black, Asian, and Mexican students, she experienced an incident that prompted these comments, "I accidentally bumped into a black girl on my way to class because I was late, and she started screaming at me about how I ran into her because she was black, and about how my people enslaved her people, and she threw her brush at me, and I was befuddled. . . . I was so frustrated at her ignorance, and at her willingness to blindly pin her problems on me, just because of the color of my skin."

Jessica Lyons, another Portland teenager, has a different view of how students of diverse backgrounds relate in her school. She reports,

> *All the races get along pretty well. Although if you just walked into our school you would not think so. Most of the white kids hang with all whites and most of the black kids hang with their black friends. We do like each other though. [Once] we actually had a Portland Public School representative come to our school and tell one of our teachers our school has too much racism. He thought this because when going through the halls you can see the split in color. But . . . behind the scenes we are all very good friends and enjoy each other very much.*[4]

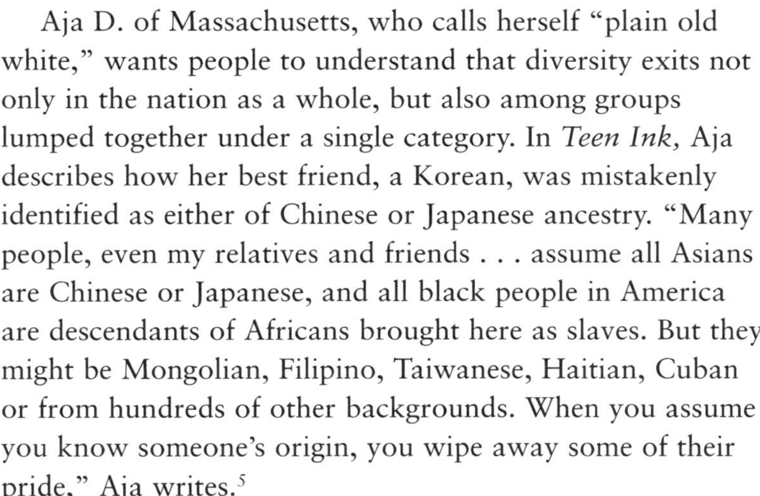

Aja D. of Massachusetts, who calls herself "plain old white," wants people to understand that diversity exits not only in the nation as a whole, but also among groups lumped together under a single category. In *Teen Ink,* Aja describes how her best friend, a Korean, was mistakenly identified as either of Chinese or Japanese ancestry. "Many people, even my relatives and friends . . . assume all Asians are Chinese or Japanese, and all black people in America are descendants of Africans brought here as slaves. But they might be Mongolian, Filipino, Taiwanese, Haitian, Cuban or from hundreds of other backgrounds. When you assume you know someone's origin, you wipe away some of their pride," Aja writes.[5]

Being judged and categorized by classmates is common for many teenagers of mixed heritage. Seventeen-year-old Chad Morgan of Indiana notes that "it's hard for some black people to fully accept me into their world. [I'm] not black enough to have dealt with the things they have. I have to be black for them and white for the white people."[6]

Veronica of Lansing, Michigan, is of white/Hungarian and African/French ancestry. When she was in high school during the mid-1990s, Veronica says that nearly every day at school someone would ask her: "Are you Mexican, Indian,

Puerto Rican?" Her classmates wanted to know where she came from, whether she was born in the United States, and what she called herself. Other teenagers couldn't "figure out who I am because of my skin color and hair—somebody always want[ed] to feel my hair," Veronica says. She explains that she was also subjected to teasing and taunts because most of her friends were white. Some black teenagers called her a "wannabe," not understanding that, as she notes, "I am part white—it has nothing to do with wanting to be."[7]

Eighteen-year-old Valerie Kruley, who lives in Oak Park, Illinois, a Chicago suburb, is also of mixed heritage—African American and Caucasian—and is Jewish. She notes that she has "experienced prejudice because of both skin color and religion" and has been accused of "not being black enough" and "not being Jewish enough." But she writes that being biracial has not been a big issue in her life, even though many people believe that biracial young people have psychological problems and a difficult time adapting. "I know that many biracial people feel like they don't belong and they have a hard time finding a group of friends who will accept them, but there are those of us who have the opposite reaction." Valerie declares:

> *If you grow up in an accepting, diversified place like Oak Park, it's not as difficult for the child. I have lived a very easy life because of that, and how well my parents raised me.*
>
> *Oak Park is known for its diversity—both the school and the neighborhood. I think the neighborhood of Oak Park does a good job of celebrating the many different cultures, which is a major reason why my parents chose to move here. It has an annual ethnic fest and various social clubs to join, and generally is a very accepting neighborhood. I've never felt unwelcome or uncomfortable. . . . I've never felt as if I didn't belong. The school, Oak Park and River Forest High School (OPRF), is also very diversified. . . . [However,] though there are many different cultures present at OPRF, there is somewhat of a separation, especially between the African Americans*

and the Caucasians. If you walk in the cafeteria, there are apparent separate tables for each race. . . . [Yet] races do mix. There are Caucasians who are friends with the African Americans, and vice versa. My best friend happens to be Puerto Rican and Filipino.[8]

READ ALL ABOUT IT!

Psychologist Beverly Daniel Tatum wrote the book *"Why Are All the Black Kids Sitting Together in the Cafeteria?" and Other Conversations about Race* because so many students, educators, and parents have asked her the question posed in the title. As Tatum points out, "Walk into any racially mixed high school cafeteria at lunch time and you will instantly notice that in the sea of adolescent faces, there is an identifiable group of black students sitting together. Conversely . . . there are many groups of white students sitting together as well, though people rarely comment about that."[9]

Tatum explains how young people establish and affirm their racial and ethnic identities, which may include being with others of the same heritage. For black students that may mean sitting together at the cafeteria table where they can safely tell each other about racist behavior they have encountered. In Tatum's words, "We need to understand that in a racially mixed setting, racial grouping is a developmental process in response to an environmental stressor, racism. Joining with one's peers for support in the face of stress is a positive coping strategy. What is problematic is that the young people are operating with a very limited definition of what it means to be black, based largely on cultural stereotypes."[10]

Although the book includes some psychological terms and concepts, for the most part it is written in an easy-to-understand manner with a conversational tone. Tatum uses quotes from numerous students and describes their experiences. She provides practical suggestions in the last chapter on how to engage in cross-racial dialogue. [Beverly Daniel Tatum, *"Why Are All the Black Kids Sitting Together in the Cafeteria?" and Other Conversations about Race*, rev. ed. (New York: Basic, 1999)]

UNDERSTANDING DIFFERENCES

Growing up in a "diversified place," as Valerie calls Oak Park, is not possible for many Americans. But there are numerous opportunities to learn about diverse cultures. A start is reading books and seeing movies or videos about ethnic groups, sexual orientation, or gender differences.

Another possibility is becoming a participant in the Anytown USA program described earlier. Weekend retreats to expand awareness of multiculturalism may be offered at some colleges or by civic groups. Exchange programs are also helpful. For example, a church group might exchange visits with a group from a synagogue or temple. A student group from a predominantly black or Hispanic school might change places with a group from a predominantly white school.

In teenager Katie Robert's opinion, people could easily get firsthand knowledge about cultures different from their own by doing "community work, by helping other cultures get by and make a living." People who are new in a community "hardly know anyone and could use some help and friends."[11]

Middle and senior high schools frequently have diversity programs integrated into the curriculum to help promote understanding and appreciation of varied cultural traditions, attitudes, and values represented in the school community. Activities may include assembly programs that teach tolerance and cooperative living. Perhaps an International Night might involve an evening of food, music, and dance. Special cultural events such as Black History Month, Chinese New Year, Gay Pride Day, Filipino Discovery Day, Indian Spring Festival, or International Women's Day may be celebrated. Students might participate in a letter exchange program with young people in another country.

School and civic events are common means to learn about and develop respect for diverse cultures. But some people want to put their knowledge to use and take action. Where do they begin? What can a group or individual do? One of the first steps is to speak out against discrimination, bigotry, and racism.

READ ALL ABOUT IT!

Geek, nerd, wannabe, freak, jock, preppie, techie, goth, homie-g, teen-queen, and numerous racial and ethnic slurs are just some of the labels teenagers use on a daily basis. But Aisha Muharrar, in her book *More Than a Label: Why What You Wear or Who You're with Doesn't Define Who You Are*, explains how labels stereotype people and frequently hurt them. Aisha wrote this book when she was seventeen and a high school senior. She uses her own experiences and insights and includes first-person stories from some of the more than one thousand teenagers who responded to her survey about labels and labeling. The teens who are quoted live in big cities, small towns, suburbs, and rural areas across America, and they report on how it feels to be labeled and whether they label their peers. Labeling limits a person's opportunities to get to know someone, Aisha contends. A "label in your mind already speaks volumes. You end up excluding whole groups of people . . . Or they end up excluding you."[12]

During an interview on Teentalknetwork, Aisha explained to her hosts that in high school "[l]abels have become like cafeteria food . . . part of high school life. . . . [The food is] bad but no one does anything about it." The third part of her book explains how to go beyond labeling, and she reminds readers that the Golden Rule still applies. "Think how labels affect you—understand how others feel about it," she says. In her interview, she acknowledged that sometimes "a label will pop up" in her mind and she has to remind herself "to stop relying on that label and get to know the person." She urged teenagers to find out who they really are and have confidence in their individuality—to separate themselves from their labels.[13] [Aisha Muharrar, *More Than a Label: Why What You Wear or Who You're with Doesn't Define Who You Are* (Minneapolis, Minn.: Free Spirit, 2002).]

9 Speaking Out

After a Ku Klux Klan rally in northern Indiana during the summer of 2002, an editorial in a local newspaper reminded readers, "When racism puts on a Klan label, it's not hard to see. Anyone can spot bigotry if it wears a hood. But the kind of prejudice that's heard routinely doesn't come from Klan members. It's expressed by friends and family members, and too often it's passed off with a sign of agreement or a joke. Bias is found in the attitudes of employers and co-workers, in teachers and police officers, on streets and in homes. That's the kind of bigotry that has to be dealt with every day."[1]

Dealing with "everyday bigotry and racism" often begins with the recognition that everyone to some extent has certain

I think that so much has and is being done to promote cultural acceptance in America. Most cities have ethnic festivals, or similar events, and I think these programs are very beneficial. . . . We should join together to celebrate our American heritage and the heritage of all the other nationalities of which America is comprised.

—Teenager Chad Morgan

THE VALUE OF A VOICE

The words attributed to a German minister, Martin Niemöller (1892–1984), have been quoted frequently to show the value of speaking out. Niemöller, a Lutheran, was arrested by the Nazi Gestapo in 1938 and was sent to the Dachau concentration camp. The Allied forces liberated the camp in 1945, and some time later a student asked Niemöller how his imprisonment could have happened. Niemöller explained:

In Germany they came first for the Communists, and I didn't speak up because I wasn't a Communist. Then they came for the Jews, and I didn't speak up because I wasn't a Jew. Then they came for the trade unionists, and I didn't speak up because I wasn't a trade unionist. Then they came for the Catholics, and I didn't speak up because I was a Protestant. Then they came for me, and by that time no one was left to speak up.[2]

prejudices and stereotypical views. For example, it's common to judge people on the basis of their appearance, clothing, or speech. But that does not mean a person with prejudices is automatically "bad" or cannot change her or his ideas. So, individuals need to examine their own attitudes before trying to persuade others that tolerance and respect for diversity are worthwhile. Then, it may be possible to stand up to friends, relatives, classmates, teachers, and others.

Check it out!

The Public Eye website of Political Research Associates promotes an open, democratic, and pluralistic society. It has a running banner that points out "threats to democracy and diversity," which include anti-Semitism, bigotry, discrimination, ethnocentrism, heterosexism, militarism, neo-Nazism, prejudice, racism, scapegoating, sexism, stereotyping, and more.

FINDING A VOICE

In metropolitan Atlanta, Georgia, teenagers have an opportunity to learn how to make their opinions known regarding social issues in a Youth Communication (YC) program, patterned after similar projects in other major cities, such as Chicago, New York, San Francisco, and Washington, D.C. Atlanta YC was initiated in 1993 and incorporated by thirteen teenagers and ten adults responding to a call "to let kids 'use pencils as weapons of change.'" As a result, a newspaper called *VOX* (meaning "voice" in Latin) by and for teenagers began publication. According to the *VOX* website, the communication program "responds to the sense of powerlessness that youth, especially minority and disadvantaged youth, feel every day. . . . *VOX* has become a widely-used forum for teenagers to offer their peers information, a forum for expression . . . and involves teenagers as active citizens in the Atlanta community by circulating their ideas and voices."[3]

Tiffany Polk is one participant in the *VOX* program. She attended Walton, a "predominantly Caucasian high school" where she was among the 3 to 4 percent of African Americans in the student population. In an article for the newspaper, Tiffany wrote:

It is a tradition at my school for any students and teachers who wish to participate to wear costumes for

Halloween. A lot of people have really creative, funny, or cute costumes, and it is usually an interesting day.

However, some of the students were out of line. . . . About eight students dressed up as "black people" and one or two dressed up as "Mexicans." They put iodine and black paint on their faces in order to make their complexions darker. They wore baggy clothes and acted like what they call "ghetto" by playing rap music and speaking "Ebonics." For their "Mexican" costumes they also painted their faces darker, wore sombreros, and acted like they were speaking "Mexican slang." They walked around in that getup all day and acted what they stereotypically believe African Americans and Mexicans to be. . . . Many students, including myself, were incredibly angered and upset. We were also hurt—hurt by the actions of kids who are supposed to be our friends and classmates, and hurt by the inaction and insensitivity on the behalf of the administration.

In her article, Tiffany included the opinion of eighteen-year-old Chelsea Michelson, who described the incident as "a very mindless act. In reality it was not funny. It was very distasteful and disrespectful. It said a lot about the people who did that. It's sad that that kind of thing still goes on. Their friends didn't even have the courage to stand up to them at all and let them know how stupid that was."[4]

Another way that teenagers across the United States empower themselves to speak out and make positive changes in their communities is to take part in programs of the Do Something organization. Actor and cofounder Andrew Shue declared in testimony before a U.S. congressional subcommittee on education that "Do Something was founded on the belief that young people have the energy, idealism and power to transform our communities." In 1997, Do Something launched a Kindness and Justice Challenge, a program that encourages students to perform acts of kindness and justice for two weeks in honor of the Martin Luther King Jr. national holiday. He provided examples, documented in fifty states, of the varied acts students performed, from feeding the hungry to reaching out to those whose backgrounds were different from their own. "Students learn important values like respect, compassion, responsibility, nonviolence, and good citizenship—and put these values into practice by performing positive acts." The activities help unite students of varied races, backgrounds, and social circles, Shue testified. As part of his testimony, he read a letter from Gina, a seventeen-year-old from Tennessee, who was involved in the program:

> *My dream is that we all learn to love one another regardless of race, religion, gender, or sexual preference. My dream is that we learn to hold our brother's hand instead of holding him down, that we learn to pull people up instead of putting people down. We have to make this dream a reality because the only way for us to live to our full potential in the twenty-first century is by working and living together as brothers and sisters. We can make this dream a reality by doing the small things: smiling at a stranger, listening as they cry, volunteering with the less fortunate, standing up in the face of discrimination or eating lunch with the girl no one seems to care about. . . . We can make this dream a reality, we have to, so that America's spirit, and thus its greatness, never dies.*[5]

Tolerance.org, a Web project of the Southern Poverty Law Center, encourages people from all walks of life to fight hate and promote tolerance. A recent Tolerance.org program for teenagers is called "Mix It Up," a national campaign to encourage young people to cross group boundaries in their daily lives. One effort initiated in 2002 was "Mix It Up at Lunch Day," which aimed to get teenagers to promote change in the way students segregate themselves in the school cafeteria. Students are encouraged to get their friends to venture outside their "comfort zone" to mix it up and sit someplace new during lunch time. The Mix It Up campaign also provides opportunities for teenagers to tell their stories about cross-cultural friendships or how they got beyond cultural barriers.

A friendly handshake may be one of the first steps in closing a cultural divide. Photo by the author.

HOW TO BEGIN

It's not necessarily easy to speak out against prejudice and bigotry. And often it's difficult to know how to begin. A few suggestions might help:

- Educate others about prejudice and the negative impact it can have.
- When people make disparaging jokes or comments about groups different from their own, don't agree just to get along; offset prejudicial remarks with positive comments.
- Monitor television (TV) programs, videos, and films that portray people in a stereotypical manner and write to producers to protest such stereotypes.
- Find ways, such as organizing a civil rights team or a gay-straight alliance, to bring people of diverse backgrounds together to make changes in a school or community.
- If hate graffiti is a problem in your neighborhood, create a plan with friends or classmates to remove it.
- Report serious harassment to a trusted authority. If no action is taken, make a report again to a person who will respond appropriately. Ignoring prejudicial behavior can set the stage for violence.
- Organize a support group for anyone who is a victim of harassment or violence motivated by hate.

During the 1990s, Brian Harris, a teenager of mixed-race ancestry, often appeared on TV and radio talk shows in southern California and spoke before civic and school groups about his view that cultural and racial diversity should be celebrated. He formed an international pen-pal club and within a few months had received over five thousand responses from teenagers and adults who wanted to get to know people of diverse heritage. He once told a reporter, "I know that people of different races and cultures can live together in peace because we do it in my house. If people would just . . . treat everyone with respect, a lot of our problems would disappear. It's hard enough to have good relationships without creating all sorts of additional barriers," such as clashes over cultural differences.[6]

Chapter Notes

CHAPTER 1

1. Zainab, "The American Way?" SHiNE: Action: Take a Stand, www.shine.com/action_takeastand.cfm?content_id=american_way (accessed 30 October 2002).
2. Ad Council, "I Am an American," 17 February 2002, http://racerelations.about.com/library/weekly/aa021702a.htm (accessed 30 October 2002).
3. Anti-Defamation League, "ADL Says Pro-Palestinian Rallies Turn into Forums for Anti-Semitism," Press Release, 14 May 2002.
4. Anonymous, "Skin Color Shouldn't Be Used As a Label," *Voices Reading Eagle,* 18 June 2002, 15.
5. Cierra Benton, e-mail to the author, March 2002.
6. Dean Hamilton, interview with the author, Newport Richey, Fla., November 2002.
7. Christine I. Bennett, *Comprehensive Multicultural Education: Theory and Practice,* 2nd ed. (Boston: Allyn and Bacon, 1990), 88–89.
8. Quoted in Bennett, *Comprehensive Multicultural Education,* 89.
9. Roger Daniels, *Asian America: Chinese and Japanese in the United States since 1850* (Seattle: University of Washington Press, 1988), cited in David M. Reimers, *Unwelcome Strangers: American Identity and the Turn against Immigration* (New York: Columbia University Press, 1998), 12.
10. Bennett, *Comprehensive Multicultural Education,* 87.
11. Ameesha Nanwani, "Commitment to America," Thirteen Ed Online, 2001 Teen Leadership Institute Scholarship Essay, Second Prize Winner, www.thirteen.org/edonline/tli/2ndprize2001.htm (accessed 30 October 2002).

CHAPTER 2

1. Anonymous e-mail, "Immigrants, Not Americans, Must Adapt," no date.

2. Kara Lingenfelter, "Immigrants, Not Americans, Must Adapt: Let's Stop and Think about That!" no date, www.accs.net/users/wolf/only157.htm (accessed 30 October 2002).

3. R. P. Nettlehorst, "Notes on the Founding Fathers and the Separation of Church and State," *Quartz Hill Journal of Theology,* 23 September 1999, www.theology.edu/journal/volume2/ushistor.htm (accessed 30 October 2002).

4. Thomas Paine, *The Age of Reason* (Buffalo, N.Y.: Prometheus, 1984), 8–9; see also www.ushistory.org/paine/reason/reason1.htm (accessed 30 October 2002).

5. Yale Law School, "The Avalon Project: The Barbary Treaties 1786–1816" (original in Arabic), www.yale.edu/lawweb/avalon/diplomacy/barbary/bar1796t.htm (accessed 30 October 2002); see also Robert Boston, "Joel Barlow and the Treaty with Tripoli," *Church and State Magazine* (June 1997); Charles I. Bevans, ed., *Treaties and Other International Agreements of the United States of America, 1776–1949,* vol. 11, *Philippines–United Arab Republic* (Washington, D.C.: Department of State Publications, 1974), 1072.

6. Willard Sterne Randall, *Thomas Jefferson: A Life* (New York: HarperCollins, 1994), 203.

7. U.S. Treasury, "Fact Sheet on the History of 'In God We Trust,'" no date, www.ustreas.gov/education/fact-sheets/currency/in-god-we-trust.html (accessed 30 October 2002).

8. Kate G., "Opinion: Political Correctness," *Teen Ink* (May 2002), www.teenink.com/Past/2002/May/Opinion/Political Correctness.html (accessed 30 October 2002).

9. CNN, "Ground Zero Statue Criticized for 'Political Correctness,'" 12 January 2002.

10. Stephanie W., "Opinion: A Changing World," *Teen Ink* (May 2002), www.teenink.com/Past/2002/May/Opinion/AChanging World.html (accessed 30 October 2002).

11. Kenneth Prewitt, "Demography, Diversity, and Democracy: The 2000 Census Story," *Brookings Review* (winter 2002): 6–9.

12. Jennifer Henderson, letter to the author, May 2002.

13. Quoted in Marilyn Gardner, "Refugees Change the Face of the Heartland," *Christian Science Monitor,* 1 May 2002,

www.csmonitor.com/2002/0501/p14s01-lihc.html (accessed 30 October 2002).

14. Quoted in Gardner, "Refugees Change the Face of the Heartland."

CHAPTER 3

1. Quoted in Kathlyn Gay, *Bigotry* (Hillside, N.J.: Enslow, 1989), 9.

2. Anonymous, interview with the author, Zion, Ill., July 2002.

3. Anonymous, interview with the author, South Bend, Ind., January 1989.

4. Kristen U., "Pride and Prejudice: Twisted Views," *Teen Ink* (December 2001), http://teenink.com/Past/2001/December/Pride/TwistedViews.html (accessed 30 October 2002).

5. Graham Brink, "Lesbian Teen Sues over Required Yearbook Attire," *St. Petersburg Times,* 20 June 2002, 3B.

6. Jim Carnes, *Us and Them: A History of Intolerance in America* (Montgomery, Ala.: Southern Poverty Law Center, Teaching Tolerance Project, 1995), 113.

7. Quoted in Rhonda Parks, "Helping Teachers Help Students," *Santa Barbara News-Press,* 20 August 2001, www.youth.org/loco/PERSONProject/Alerts/States/California/training.html (accessed 30 October 2002).

8. Anonymous, "Pride and Prejudice: Hate," *Teen Ink* (April 2002), http://teenink.com/Past/2002/April/Pride/Hate.html (accessed 30 October 2002).

9. Katie Bacon, interview with Steve Olson, *Atlantic Unbound,* 26 April 2002, www.theatlantic.com/unbound/interviews/int2002-04-26.htm (accessed 30 October 2002).

10. Quoted in Natalie Angier, "Do Races Differ? Not Really, DNA Shows," *New York Times,* 22 August 2000, F4–5, www.nytimes.com/library/national/science/082200sci-genetics-race.htmlsci-genetics-race.html (accessed 16 June 2002).

11. Beverly Daniel Tatum, *"Why Are All the Black Kids Sitting Together in the Cafeteria?" and Other Conversations about Race* (New York: Basic, 1999), 7.

12. Jennifer Lynn Tweedie, e-mail to the author, April 2002.

13. Tweedie, e-mail to the author.

14. Cierra Benton, e-mail to the author, March 2002.

15. Anonymous, "The Outsider," *Teen Ink* (June 2002), http://teenink.com/Past/2002/June/Pride/TheOutsider.html (accessed 30 October 2002).

16. Quoted in Yvette Cabrera, "Student Summons the Courage to Battle Intolerance," *The Orange County Register* (InfoTrac version), 11 June 2001.

17. Cynthia, Iselda, Ezequiel, and Albert, "Migrant Workers' Children" (a student website maintained by Ricki Peto), no date, http://users.owt.com/rpeto/migrant/migrant.html (accessed 6 December 2002).

18. Marion Moses, "Farm Workers and Pesticides," in *Confronting Environmental Racism,* ed. Robert D. Bullard (Boston: South End, 1993), 161–65.

19. Quoted in Bill Maxwell, "The Real-Life Lessons about the Plight of Migrant Farm Workers," *St. Petersburg Times,* Op-Ed, 14 April 2002.

20. Robert Jensen, "White Privilege Shapes the U.S.," *Baltimore Sun,* 19 July 1998, C1, http://uts.cc.utexas.edu/~rjensen/freelance/whiteprivilege.htm (accessed 30 October 2002).

21. Peter Pae, "Chicken Plant Jobs Open U.S. Doors for Koreans," *Washington Post,* 1 December 1999, A1.

CHAPTER 4

1. Quoted in Kathlyn Gay, *"I Am Who I Am": Speaking out about Multiracial Identity* (New York: Franklin Watts, 1995), 73.

2. Children and the Media Program, *A Different World: Native American Children's Perceptions of Race and Class in the Media* (Oakland, Calif.: Children Now, 1999), 3, 5.

3. Michael A. Dorris, foreword to *American Indian Stereotypes in the World of Children: A Reader and Bibliography,* by Arlene Hirschfelder, Paulette Fairbanks Molin, and Yvonne Wakim, 2nd ed. (Lanham, Md.: Scarecrow, 1999), vii.

4. Jennifer Lynn Tweedie, e-mail to the author, April 2002.

5. Chasco Fiesta, New Port Richey, Pasco County, Florida, 2002, www.ChascoFiesta.net (accessed 30 October 2002).

6. Statements during an AIM Town Forum at the New Port Richey Public Library, New Port Richey, Florida, 25 February 2002.

7. Statements during an AIM Town Forum.

8. General Assembly, National Congress of American Indians, Executive Council Winter Session, February 25–27, 2002, Washington, D.C., "Resolution: The Elimination of New Port Richey's 'Chasco Indian Festival.'"

9. Cornel Pewewardy, "Why Educators Can't Ignore Indian Mascots," no date, www.aics.org/mascot/cornel.html (accessed 30 October 2002).

10. Jim Doyle, "Rights Panel Urges End to Indian Mascots," *San Francisco Chronicle,* 14 April 2001, A3.

11. David Pilgrim, "The Coon Caricature" (October 2000), www.ferris.edu/news/jimcrow/coon/ (accessed 30 October 2002).

12. Quoted in "About the Jim Crow Museum," *Crimson and Gold* (winter 1999), www.ferris.edu/news/jimcrow/more.htm (accessed 30 October 2002).

13. Quoted in "About the Jim Crow Museum."

14. B. Lee Artz, "Hegemony in Black and White: Interracial Buddy Films and the New Racism," in *Cultural Diversity and the U.S. Media,* ed. Yahya R. Kamalipour and Theresa Carilli (Albany: SUNY Press, 1998), 67–77.

15. Anti-Defamation League, "Anti-Semitism on the Rise in America," Press Release, 11 June 2002.

16. *Detroit Free Press* and Knight Ridder, "100 Questions and Answers about Arab Americans: A Journalist's Guide," 2001, 7.

17. *Detroit Free Press* and Knight Ridder, "100 Questions and Answers about Arab Americans: A Journalist's Guide," 6.

CHAPTER 5

1. Quoted in "My God Is Better Than Your God," in *City Kids Speak on Prejudice* (New York: Random House, 1994).

2. Jeffery L. Sheler et al., "Faith in America," *U.S. News and World Report,* 6 May 2002, 40.

3. Anonymous, "Being a Religious Minority," 10 January 2001, www.iemily.com/articleprint.cfm?ArtID=621 (accessed 6 December 2002).

4. Anonymous, "Being a Religious Minority."

5. Quoted in Tolerance.org, "Hate in the News: Graham's Anti-Islamic Comments Spark Controversy," 20 November 2001, www.tolerance.org/news/article_hate.jsp?id=337 (accessed 30 September 2002).

6. Franklin Graham, "My View of Islam," *Wall Street Journal,* 9 December 2001, Op-Ed, www.opinionjournal.com/extra/?id=95001576 (accessed 30 October 2002).

7. Quoted in The Interfaith Alliance, "Christian Coalition Head Blames Muslims for Slavery," Press Release, 29 October 1997.

8. General Board of the American Baptist Churches USA, "Anti-Muslim and Anti-Arab Prejudice in the United States of America," 18 November 2001, www.abcusa-unity.org/DeclAntiIslam.html (accessed 30 October 2002).

9. Quoted in The Interfaith Alliance, "Christian Coalition Head Blames Muslims for Slavery."

10. *Engel v. Vitale,* 370 U.S. 421 no. 468 (1962), www.lihistory.com/vault/hs817pr2.htm (accessed 30 October 2002).

11. *Lee et al. v. Weisman,* no. 90–1014 (1992), http://supct.law.cornell.edu/supct/html/90-1014.ZS.html (accessed 30 October 2002).

12. See U.S. Supreme Court decisions on religious liberty and schools on the Internet at http://supct.law.cornell.edu/supct/ (accessed 30 October 2002) and at www.supremecourtus.gov/ (accessed 30 October 2002).

13. Quoted in Americans United for Separation of Church and State, "Public Schools Can't Require Flag Pledge with 'Under God' in It, Federal Court Rules," Press Release, 26 June 2002.

14. "PFAW President, Ralph G. Neas, Addresses Divisive Comments by Religious Right Leaders," Press Release, 13 September 2001, www.pfaw.org/pfaw/general/default.aspx?oid=1817 (accessed 30 October 2002).

CHAPTER 6

1. Terrell Jones, "Are We Really Penn State?" Office of Public Information, Pennsylvania State University, Op-Ed Program, 25 October 2000, www.psu.edu/ur/oped/jones.html (accessed 30 October 2002).

2. Kandea Mosley, "3 Charged with Ithaca Racial Assault," *Ithaca Journal,* 11 July 2002, www.civilrights.org/library/detail.cfm?id=9479 (accessed 7 December 2002).

3. Bob Egelko and Christopher Heredia, "Hate Charges Filed in Slaying of 2 Lesbians," *San Francisco Chronicle,* 11 April 2002, www.sfgate.com/cgi-bin/article.cgi?f=/c/a/2002/04/11/MN47487.DTL (accessed 30 October 2002).

4. National Asian Pacific American Legal Consortium, "Backlash: When America Turned on Its Own," Executive Summary, 2002.

5. "For the Record," *Intelligence Report* (summer 2002): 62.

6. See www.twelvearyannations.com/anyac.html (accessed 30 October 2002).

7. Anti-Defamation League, "Hate on the Internet" (October 1998), www.adl.org/special%5Freports/hate%5Fon%5Fwww/print.asp (accessed 4 November, 2002).

8. Kathlyn Gay, *Neo-Nazis: A Growing Threat* (Springfield, N.J.: Enslow, 1997), 26–35; see also Sandra D. Leek, ed., *A Profile of Extremist Movements in America,* 4th ed. (Indianapolis: Indiana Civil Rights Commission, 1999), 28; and Anti-Defamation League, "Aryan Nations," Press Release, 2 March 1998, www.adl.org/presrele/neosk_82/aryan_nations_82.asp (accessed 30 October 2002).

9. Tom Dolan, "Kidnap Suspect Arrested," *The Elkhart Truth,* 4 January 2002, www.elktruth.com/news/276206881106244.bsp (accessed 30 October 2002).

10. See www.adl.org/learn/ext_us/Metzger.asp (accessed 30 October 2002).

11. U.S. Department of Education, Office of Elementary and Secondary Education Safe and Drug-free Schools Program, "Preventing Youth Hate Crime" (1997), www.ed.gov/pubs/HateCrime/start.html (accessed 30 October 2002).

12. Quoted in Marshall V. King, "Former Racist Talks about Hate Groups," *The Elkhart Truth,* 21 November 2001, www.elktruth.com/news/276224474634504.bsp (accessed 30 October 2002).

13. Quoted in King, "Former Racist Talks about Hate Groups"; see also Germantown Academy, "Ex–Aryan Nation Propagandist Warns GA Students about Hate Groups," Press Release, 23 February 2001, www.ga.k12.pa.us/development/PressRelease/00-01/Cochrane.htm (accessed 30 October 2002).

14. Center for New Community and Southern Poverty Law Center's *Intelligence Report,* "White Power Bands," January 2002, www.tolerance.org/news/article_hate.jsp?id=403 (accessed 30 October 2002).

15. Devin Burghart, ed., *Soundtracks to the White Revolution: White Supremacist Assaults on Youth Music Subcultures* (Chicago: Center for New Community, 1999), 88.

16. Tolerance.org, "Present at the Creation" (January 2001), www.tolerance.org/news/article_hate.jsp?id=402 (accessed 30 October 2002).

17. Tolerance.org, "Present at the Creation."

18. Resistance Records, "Ethnic Cleansing: The Game," www.resistance.com/ethniccleansing/catalog.htm (accessed 30 October 2002).

19. Anti-Defamation League, "ADL Report: Growing Proliferation of Racist Video Games Target Youth on The Internet," Press Release, 19 February 2002, www.adl.org/PresRele/extremism_72/4042_72.asp (accessed 30 October 2002).

20. Quoted in Justin Leighty, "Witmer Admits Guilt," *The Elkhart Truth,* 12 January 2002, www.elktruth.com/news/276222110410048.bsp (accessed 30 October 2002).

CHAPTER 7

1. Quoted in Noreen S. Ahmed-Ullah, "In Chinatown, a Principal Unites 2 Cultures," *Chicago Tribune,* 10 July 2001.

2. National Conference for Community and Justice, Greater Atlanta Region, no date, www.nccj-atlanta.org/programs_anytown.asp (accessed 30 October 2002).

3. Nicole Ashby, U.S. Department of Education, "ANYTOWN—Community Program Changes Tampa Youth from the Inside Out," *Community Update* (August 2001), www.ed.gov/offices/OIIA/communityupdate/08-2001/anytown.html (accessed 30 October 2002).

4. "Kate Crockford" profile, no date, www.stopthehate.org/get_involved/students/profile_crockford.php (accessed 30 October 2002).

5. Quoted in Victoria Scanlan Stefanakos, "The Sound of Silence," *The Advocate,* 2 April 2002, www.advocate.com/html/stories/860/860_silence.asp (accessed 30 October 2002).

6. Stefanakos, "Sound of Silence."

7. Stefanakos, "Sound of Silence."

8. Idaho Human Rights Commission, "Idaho Human Rights Organizations Announce Anti-hate Poster Campaign," Press Release, 29 May 2001, www.humanrightsidaho.org/news.html (accessed 30 October 2002).

9. Kathlyn Gay, *Neo-Nazis: A Growing Threat* (Springfield, N.J.: Enslow, 1997), 99.

10. See www.pbs.org/niot (accessed 30 October 2002).

11. BookMania from Stafford, Texas, "One of the Best Books I've Ever Read," *Amazon.com,* 29 November 2002, Reviews, www.amazon.com/exec/obidos/tg/detail/-/0446310786/102-4813328-7625730?vi=glance (accessed 9 December 2002).

12. Young African Americans against Media Stereotypes, "Who We Are," no date, www.yaaams.org/about.shtml (accessed 30 October 2002).

13. Quoted in Kelly Ryan Gilmer, "School's Cultural Strife Eases," *St. Petersburg Times,* 4 January 2002, www.sptimes.com/2002/01/04/SouthPinellas/School_s_cultural_str.shtml (accessed 30 October 2002).

14. "About Bridges," no date, www.und.nodak.edu/org/span/bridges/index2.html (accessed 30 October 2002).

15. U.S. Department of Justice, Office of Justice Programs, "Promising Practices against Hate Crimes" (May 2000), 22, www.ncjrs.org/pdffiles1/bja/181425.pdf (accessed 30 October 2002).

CHAPTER 8

1. Katie Roberts, letter to the author, August 2002.
2. Cierra Benton, e-mail to the author, March 2002.
3. Lisa Miller, e-mail to the author, February 2002.
4. Jessica Lyons, e-mail to the author, May 2002.
5. Aja D., "Pride and Prejudice: My Korean Friend," *Teen Ink* (January 2001), www.teenink.com/Past/2001/January/Pride/MyKoreanFriend.html (accessed 30 October 2002).
6. Chad Morgan, letter to the author, September 2002.
7. Quoted in Kathlyn Gay, *"I Am Who I Am": Speaking out about Multiracial Identity* (New York: Franklin Watts, 1995), 14.
8. Valerie Kruley, e-mail to the author, April 2002.
9. Beverly Daniel Tatum, *"Why Are All the Black Kids Sitting Together in the Cafeteria?" and Other Conversations about Race,* rev. ed. (New York: Basic, 1999), 52.
10. Tatum, *"Why Are All the Black Kids Sitting Together in the Cafeteria?"* 62.
11. Roberts, letter to the author.
12. Aisha Muharrar, *More Than a Label: Why What You Wear or Who You're with Doesn't Define Who You Are* (Minneapolis, Minn.: Free Spirit, 2002), 20.
13. Aisha Muharrar, audio interview, www.teentalknetwork.com/ct2.htm#REFERENCE.

CHAPTER 9

1. "Bigotry Here Full Time," *The Elkhart Truth,* 1 August 2002, www.elktruth.com/news/276207411763756.bsp (accessed 30 October 2002).

2. Quoted in the Jewish Virtual Library, "Martin Niemöller: The Failure to Speak Up Against the Nazis," www.us-israel.org/jsource/Holocaust/Niemoller_quote.html (accessed 16 May 2003).

3. "The History of Youth Communication," *VOX* (2002), www.youthcommunication-vox.org/history.htm (accessed 30 October 2002).

4. Tiffany Polk, "Drawing the Line between Humor and Hate," *VOX* (March 2002), 11, www.youthcommunication-vox.org/302pg10.htm (accessed 30 October 2002).

5. Quoted in Andrew Shue, Testimony before the Congressional Subcommittee to Reauthorize the Partnerships in Character Education Pilot Project Program, 1 March 2000, http://edworkforce.house.gov/hearings/106th/ecyf/charactered3100/shue.htm (accessed 30 October 2002).

6. Quoted in Jerry Holderman, "'Colorblind' Boy Shares His Place," *Los Angeles Times,* 14 October 1992, E3.

Glossary

Bigotry: Intolerance of any religious belief, culture, or race different from one's own.

Culture: The shared arts, customs, folklore, history, traditions, and values of a group of people.

Cultural diversity: Differences in race, ethnicity, language, nationality, or religion among various groups within a community, organization, or nation.

Cross-cultural: The interaction between people from two or more different cultures.

Discrimination: Prejudicial actions that may exclude or deny opportunity because of race, ethnicity, religion, gender, sexual orientation, or disability.

Ethnic: Of or relating to people linked by a common racial, national, tribal, religious, linguistic, or cultural heritage.

Ethnicity: A quality and/or classification assigned to a specific group of people connected by a common national origin or language.

Ethnocentrism: The belief that one's own race, nation, or culture is superior to all others.

Gay: A term for male homosexuals, but is often used to describe both male and female homosexuals.

Gender: Classification of people based on the social categories "men" and "women," as opposed to biological and physical differences that form the categories "male" and "female."

Harassment: Behavior intended to belittle or intimidate another person because of his or her race, ethnicity, color, religion, ancestry, national origin, or disability.

Heterosexism: A belief that heterosexuality is inherently "right" and superior to other forms of sexuality.

Homophobia: The irrational fear of homosexuals, homosexuality, or any behavior, belief, or attitude of self or others that doesn't conform to rigid sex-role stereotypes.

Immigrant: A person who comes to a nation or region to take up permanent residence.

Institutional racism: Attitudes, behaviors, and practices within an institution that subordinate persons or groups because of race or ethnic background.

Lesbian: A term for female homosexuals.

Mainstream: A term that is often used to describe a broad population that is primarily white and middle class.

Multiculturalism: The practice of acknowledging and respecting the various cultures, religions, races, ethnicities, attitudes, and opinions within a specific place.

People of color: People who identify themselves as black or African American; Hispanic, Latino, or Chicano; Asian or Pacific Islander; or American Indian or Alaskan Native.

Pluralism: A system within which individuals or groups differ in cultures and allows for the development of a common tradition, while preserving the right of each group to maintain its cultural heritage.

Stereotypes: Labels for and views about people of a certain racial, ethnic, or cultural group that contend that every member of that group behaves in the same way.

Tolerance: Acceptance and open-mindedness to practices, attitudes, and cultures different from one's own.

Xenophobia: The fear of strangers or foreigners.

For Further Information

BOOKS

Ansary, Tamim. *West of Kabul, East of New York: An Afghan American Story.* New York: Farrar, Straus and Giroux, 2002.

Barnes, Annie S. *Everyday Racism: A Book for All Americans.* Naperville, Ill.: Sourcebooks, 2000

Burghart, Devin. *Sounding Tracks to the White Revolution.* Chicago: Center for New Community, 1999.

Hong, Maria, ed. *Growing up Asian American.* New York: Avon, 1995.

Katz, William Loren. *Black Indians: A Hidden Heritage.* New York: Atheneum, 1986.

Nam, Vickie, ed. *YELL-O Girls! Emerging Voices Explore Culture, Diversity, and Growing up Asian American.* New York: Quill/HarperCollins, 2001

Tatum, Beverly Daniel. *"Why Are All the Black Kids Sitting Together in the Cafeteria?" and Other Conversations about Race.* New York: Basic, 1997.

ORGANIZATIONS

American-Arab Anti-Discrimination Committee
4201 Conn. Ave. NW, #300
Washington, DC 20008
Phone: 202-244-2990
www.adc.org

American Jewish Committee
The Jacob Blaustein Building
165 East 56th Street
New York, NY 10022-2746
Phone: 212-751-4000
http://ajc.org

Anti-Defamation League
823 United Nations Plaza
New York, NY 10017
Phone: 212-490-2525
www.adl.org

Asian American Legal Defense and Education Fund
99 Hudson St., 12th Floor
New York, NY 10013-2869
Phone: 212-966-5932
www.apa2000.org/

Center for Democratic Renewal
PO Box 50469
Atlanta, GA 30302
Phone: 404-221-0025
www.publiceye.org/index.htm

Cultural Diversity Network
104 1/2 West Broadway
Owatonna, MN 55060
Phone: 507-444-4272
www.hickorytech.net/~cdn/index.html

Global Kids
561 Broadway
New York, NY 10012
Phone: 212-226-0130
www.globalkids.org/index.shtml

National Council of Churches
475 Riverside Drive, Room 670
New York, NY 10115
Phone: 212-870-2227
www.ncccusa.org/

National Council for Community and Justice
475 Park Avenue South, 19th Floor
New York, NY 10016
Phone: 212-545-1300
www.nccj.org/

National Gay and Lesbian Task Force
1325 Massachusetts Ave NW, Suite 600
Washington, DC 20005
Phone: 202-393-5177
www.ngltf.org/main.html

Parents and Friends of Lesbians and Gays
1726 M Street, NW, Suite 400
Washington, DC 20036
Phone: 202-467-8180
www.pflag.org

People for the American Way
2000 M Street, NW
Washington, DC 20036
Phone: 202-467-4999
www.pfaw.org

Political Research Associates
1310 Broadway, Suite 201
Somerville, MA 02144
Phone: 617-666-5300
www.publiceye.org/

The Prejudice Institute
2743 Maryland Ave.
Baltimore, MD 21218
Phone: 410-243-6987
www.prejudiceinstitute.org

Southern Poverty Law Center
400 Washington Avenue
Montgomery, AL 36104
Phone: 334-956-8200
www.splcenter.org/

Study Circles Resource Center
697 Pomfret Street, Box 203
Pomfret, CT 06258
Phone: 860-928-2616
www.studycircles.org/

SELECTED WEBSITES

BRIDGES
www.und.nodak.edu/org/span/bridges/index2.html

Center for New Community
www.und.nodak.edu/org/span/bridges/index2.html

Civilrights.org
www.civilrights.org

Cultural Diversity Network
www.hickorytech.net/~cdn/index.html

Global Kids
www.globalkids.org/index.shtml

National Coalition on Racism and Sports in the Media
www.aics.org/NCRSM/index.htm

Partners against Hate
www.partnersagainsthate.org/

Stop the Hate.org
http://stop-the-hate.org/resource.html

Teen Ink Pride and Prejudice
www.teenink.com/Pride/index.html

Tolerance.org
www.tolerance.org/

Index

Abercrombie and Fitch, 47
Ad Council, 1
Adams, John, 13
The Advocate, 78, 79
African American(s), 29, 42, 45, 48, 63, 67, 82, 90–91, 96
American Indian, 7, 28, 33, 38–41. *See also* indigenous people; Native peoples
American Indian Movement, 41
Amish, 53
Anti-Defamation League (ADL), 3, 48, 57, 64–65, 69, 73, 82
Anytown USA, 76–77, 92
Arab American(s), 1, 48–50, 80
Argentina, 2
Aryan Nations, 7, 67–68, 70, 80
Asian American(s), 1, 19, 46–47

Baptist(s), 12, 56
barbarians, 26
Beaulieu, Ruby, 41
Benton, Cierra, 3, 29, 88
bigotry, 22, 50, 55–57, 75, 81–83, 92, 95–96, 99, 111
BRIDGES, 84
Burdi, George, 71–72

Canada, 2, 39, 73
caricatures, 6, 37–38, 42–43, 46–47
Caucasian, 27, 33–34, 54, 90–91, 96
Center for Democratic Renewal, 65
Center for New Community, 65, 71
Chicago, 3, 5, 29, 75, 81, 88, 90, 96
Christian Identity, 7, 67–68
Church of the Creator, 64–65, 71–72
Civil War, 13, 66
Cochran, Floyd, 70
Cultural Diversity Network, 84

Darrow, Clarence, 52, 62
Day of Silence, 78–79
deist, 13
Detroit, 3, 49, 71
Detroit Free Press, 49
disabilities, 4, 22, 29
discrimination, 6, 14, 22, 29, 60; against African American(s), 30; against homosexuals, 24–26, 60, 78–79; against Japanese Americans, 8; against Mexicans, 30; against migrant workers, 31–32; against Mormon, 54; confronting, 82–83, 90, 96, 98; definition, 111; in housing, 23
Doerzapf, Jessica, 25
dwarfism, 22

E Pluribus Unum, 1, 3
ethnocentrism, 21–22, 96
European explorers, 21, 39
evolution, 52, 62

Falwell, Rev. Jerry, 61
Foxman, Abraham H., 48, 73
France, 2

Gay Straight Alliance, 77
Genesis, 57
genocide, 3, 60–61
Germany, 2–3, 18, 94
graffiti, 2, 70, 79–80, 99
Graham, Franklin, 55
Graham, Rev. Billy, 55
Greeks, 18, 21, 26

Hamilton, Dean, 5
harassment, 24–26, 49, 70, 78, 81, 99
Harris, Brian, 100
hate crime(s), 1, 64, 70, 73–76, 81, 85
hate group(s), 64–71, 73
hate mail, 63
Henderson, Jennifer, 17
Hertzberg, Rabbi Arthur, 56
Hispanic, 14, 83–84, 92
Hitler, Adolf, 3, 67, 69
Holocaust, 3, 65, 73, 77
homosexual(s), 7, 24–26, 60, 65, 68, 111–12

immigrant(s), 5, 67, 112; anti-, 11; Bavarian, 18; Chinese, 7; European, 6–7; Jewish, 48; Mexican, 34; nation of, 4; recent, 16, 37; as scapegoats, 34; Somalian, 16–17
"In God We Trust," 11, 13
indigenous people, 7, 18, 21, 27, 38–42
Intelligence Report, 71, 82
Islam, 50, 55–57, 65
Israelis, 2

Japanese Americans, 7–8
Jefferson, Thomas, 13
Jews, 3, 7, 48, 51, 53, 58, 65, 67–69, 72–73, 80, 95
Jim Crow Museum of Racist Memorabilia, 43
Judaism, 2, 50

Kaplan, Roy, 77, 83
King, Rodney, 87
Kruley, Valerie, 90
Ku Klux Klan (KKK), 1, 7, 44, 64, 66–67, 70

Latinos/Latinas, 42, 46–48
Lyons, Jessica, 89

Mapping Human History, 26
Massachusetts' Governor's Task Force on Hate Crimes, 81
McVeigh, Timothy, 70
melting pot, 4, 6–8
Metzger, Tom, 68
Mexican(s), 30–32, 34, 46–47, 88–89, 97
migrant worker(s), 31–32
Miller, Lisa, 88
minstrel show, 43
Mix It Up campaign, 97
mixed-race, 4, 37, 100
More Than A Label: Why What You Wear or Who You're With Doesn't Define Who You Are, 93
Morgan, Chad, 89, 95
Mormon(s), 54, 57
multicultural, 11–12, 22, 47
multiculturalism, 92, 112

Murphy, Sheridan, 41
Muslim(s), 1–3, 17, 48, 50, 53, 55–56, 58, 83

Nanwani, Ameesha, 8
National Alliance, 69, 73
National Asian Pacific American Legal Consortium, 63, 65
National Association for the Advancement of Colored People (NAACP), 45, 65, 83
National Conference for Community and Justice, 76, 83
Native Americans, 7, 38. *See also* American Indian(s); Native peoples
Native people(s), 37–39, 41–42, 46–47, 84
neo-Nazi(s), 7, 64–65, 67, 69–71, 73
Nettelhorst, R. P., 12
"new world," 21, 27
Niemöller, Martin, 95
non-Christians, 53, 68

Olson, Steve, 26

Paine, Thomas, 13
Palestinians, 2
People for the American Way, 61
Pewewardy, Cornel, 40
Pierce, William, 69
Pilgrim, David, 43–44
Pipher, Mary, 17–18, 21
pledge of allegiance, 12, 52, 60
pluralism, 8, 112
political correctness/politically correct, 13–15
prejudice, 1, 50, 95–96; against homosexuals, 24–25; against Jews, 2, 90; against Muslims and Arabs, 56; amidst diversity, 21–22; counteracting, 2, 75–78, 81–82, 88, 99; definition, 22; perpetuating, 30, 34–35; racial, 28
Prejudice Institute, 65
Prewitt, Kenneth, 16
Protestant(s), 5, 13, 51, 95
Pulzetti, Maria, 78

Quakers, 51

racism, 33, 89, 95; amidst diversity, 21; anti-, 56, 72, 96; basis for, 22; definition of, 26, 28; denial of, 29; experienced by African Americans, 29, 44–46, 62, 91; experienced by Asian(s), 4; experienced by Native Americans, 42; institutionalized, 33, 112; perpetuated, 30, 33–35, 37; reducing, 75, 77, 83–84, 92, 95
racist images, 37, 40, 43, 47
refugee(s), 16–19
Roberts, Katie, 88
Robertson, Pat, 55–56, 61
Rockwell, George Lincoln, 69
Roman Catholic, 7
Romans, 21, 26

Sambo, 42–43
Schindler, Allen, 24
Scopes, John T., 52, 62
Seventh-Day Adventist, 52
sexual orientation, 4, 24–25, 29, 74, 91
Shepard, Matthew, 25
Shue, Andrew, 97–98
Simon Wiesenthal Center, 65, 83
skinheads, 7, 68, 80
slavery, 41–43, 55–56, 60, 84
Southern Poverty Law Center, 65–66, 82, 98

stereotype(s), 14, 22; of African American(s), 6, 42–45; of American Indians/Native peoples, 37–39, 41–42; of Arab Americans, 48–50; of Asians, 47; counteracting, 1, 77, 82, 84, 91, 93, 99; definition, 1, 112; of Jews, 47–48; of Latinos, 42, 46; of migrant workers, 31–32; perpetuating, 37; racist, 37; religious, 57

Tatum, Beverly Daniel, 28, 91
Teen Ink, 14–15, 89
Ten Ways to Fight Hate, 82
terrorist(s), 1, 9, 48, 61, 69
The Interfaith Alliance (TIA), 56
To Kill A Mockingbird, 81
The Turner Diaries, 69
Tweedie, Jennifer, 39

Unitarians, 13, 51, 53, 58
Us and Them: A History of Intolerance in America, 24
U.S. Commission on Civil Rights, 42
U.S. Constitution, 12, 51–52, 58, 62, 65, 67, 73
U.S. history, 6, 14–15, 24, 46
U.S. Supreme Court, 52–53, 58–59

vandalism, 2, 74
Venter, J. Craig, 27
Villasenor, Lizdabeth and Veronica, 30
violence, motivated by prejudice and hatred, 1–3, 55–56, 62, 70, 78, 99
VOX newspaper, 87, 95

white Anglo-Saxon Protestants (WASPS), 5, 7
White Aryan Resistance, 64, 68
white privilege, 33
white supremacist(s), 7, 64–68, 70–71, 73
Why Are All the Black Kids Sitting Together in the Cafeteria?, 91
World Trade Center, 1, 14
World War I, 7–8, 18, 65, 67
World War II, 7–8, 65, 67

Young African-Americans Against Media Stereotypes, 82
Youngblood, Nicole, 24

xenophobia, 22, 112

About the Author

Kathlyn Gay is the author of more than one hundred books that focus on social and environmental issues, culture, history, communication, and sports for a variety of audiences. Some of her books have been written in collaboration with family members. A full-time freelance author, Kathlyn has also published hundreds of magazine features and stories, plays, and promotional materials; and she has written and contributed to encyclopedias, teachers' manuals, and textbooks. She and her husband, Arthur, are Florida residents.